AMERICAN SHEET MUSIC

A Guide to Collecting Sheet Music from 1775 to 1975
With Prices

by Daniel B. Priest

WALLACE-HOMESTEAD BOOK CO.
1912 GRAND
DES MOINES, IOWA 50309

ISBN# 0-87069-205-4
Library of Congress No. 76-23905

WALLACE-HOMESTEAD BOOK CO.
1912 GRAND AVE.
DES MOINES, IOWA 50309

DEDICATION
This book is dedicated to my wife,
Lorna, who has shared the writing of this book, and my life, so lovingly.

Acknowledgments

The author is indebted to Thornton Hagert of Washington, D.C., a prominent collector and musicologist and leader of the New Sunshine Jazz Band, for his advice and for furnishing his files and collections for much of this work. A salute, also, to Julia Moed of Chevy Chase, Maryland, a perceptive antique dealer who shared her collection during the writing of this book. Mark Kinnaman was the photographer who made the black-and-white and color photographs of the sheet music covers.

About the Author

Daniel B. Priest is a collector of American sheet music, a musician and, with his wife, operates an antique business in the Washington, D.C. suburbs.

He has been involved in music since his teens when he was the co-founder of *Jazz Magazine,* a publication devoted to early American jazz music. His interest in music criticism and journalism led him to music, itself, and he took up the study of music and learned to play the cornet. Now based in Washington, he plays with the New Sunshine Jazz Band, a group of semiprofessional musicians who revere the early jazz composers and who have made three LP albums. One of the albums, "Old Rags," is distributed internationally by RCA Victor and got high praise from critics in the trade and the general press. Many of the tunes in that album, as well as many on their upcoming disc, have never been recorded before.

Author Daniel B. Priest

Priest is married to Lorna Lethbridge Priest who maintains their antique business in Kensington, Maryland. When Priest is not collecting sheet music, or playing with the New Sunshine Band, he is a public relations executive with the firm of Harshe-Rotman & Druck, Inc. The Priests live in Chevy Chase, Maryland.

THE CONTENTS

CHAPTER I

Some Definitions

In the very beginning, it would be useful to state some definitions and set the scope of this book.

It has to do with popular American sheet music from the beginning of this form in America, somewhere in the middle of the eighteenth century, to today.

What's a popular song? That's a song that is not written to be sung in a church. It is a song that does not aspire to classical company. It is a tune, a ditty, an air, a piece of music that is designed to be whistled, hummed, sung, played and performed in any way that pleases, by the American public at large. Not all songs, as writers painfully know, are popular, but it's not for lack of trying.

It isn't a lowbrow music. Good popular songs are hummed by everyone, from a classical violinist to a bricklayer. Some of the better composers; Gershwin, Richard Rodgers, Vernon Duke, for instance, have had classical training and can write respectable, serious music, themselves.

What is a popular song? It's a song written to be heard and sung by the American public. And to be enjoyed. That's all.

"Song sheets" and "piano music" are sometimes other terms for sheet music, but the term sheet music has survived and is considered by the professionals, collectors and composers alike to be the most accurate term.

CHAPTER II

A Chronology of Popular Music in America

Music reflects a culture, and the music from the colonial period was, like other aspects of the American culture, imported from England.

It had its roots in the church with a little martial spirit thrown in for seasoning. Music was, the early and proper colonists felt, for the soul and for the flag. Music for dancing and music to drink by was a bit faster of pace than the normal gait of the English transplants in the Bay Colony.

For the first 100 years or so, the culture of New England maintained the shape and color of parent England. About the middle of the eighteenth century, it began to evolve into a design that reflected the rigors of colonial life and the adventurous spirit of the Americans.

After almost a century of psalm singing and an occasional Christmas carol or two, a free-thinking and free-singing American emerged to begin the new spirit of music in the colonies.

Disdaining the now musty *Bay Psalm Book*, the first collection of songs of any sort published in America (1640), a new force appeared in New England and the changes began.

The new force was a spavined, irascible music teacher named William Billings. Before the Revolutionary War he had created his own revolution in music with a book called *The New England Psalm Singer, or, An American Chorister*. He went to the popular Bostonian silversmith and engraver, Paul Revere, to have him do the frontispiece engraving.

But, however modernized those songs were, they were still psalms, and Billings was reaching out for something more advanced. He found it in "Chester" which was sung throughout the Revolutionary War and has become America's first in a very long line of war songs. The lyrics have great power: "Let Tyrants Shake Their Iron Rod" and the song was, a Tin Pan Alley might say a century later, a smash hit.

Well, who was this Billings and how did he get that way? Billings (1746-1800) besides being our first really "successful" songwriter was also the first song plugger. He would often exhort his choir, the congregation and any within listening distance, to "Sing, everybody sing."

But before Billings can be profiled, there is an even earlier writer who must be noted. He is Francis Hopkinson (1737-1791), a signer of the Declaration of Independence and judge of the U.S. District Court. He wrote a set of lyrics to "Yankee Doodle."

Hopkinson was typical of the songwriter of that period, more poet than musician. They were essentially lyricists who borrowed melodies shamelessly from the Old Country. "Yankee Doodle" was an early favorite of the New Country and could be the most played song in the nation's history.

All of this was before ASCAP and BMI and royalties and copyright offices. The writers of that period were amateurs, but today would be classified as professionals.

When the new century dawned in what was to become the "American Century," music publishing was still a minor industry. When people sang they sang of home and hearth and the simple joys of country life.

The Star Spangled Banner Is Written

The War of 1812 burst and out of it came the national anthem, but no one was to know that for many years. Certainly not its composer, Francis Scott Key.

Key was a Baltimore lawyer who watched the shelling of Fort McHenry from a vessel anchored in Baltimore's harbor. He was so overcome by the passion of seeing his young nation's flag that he wrote the words to "The Star Spangled Banner" during the evening.

In keeping with the tradition, he had no tune, so he put the words to an English drinking song, "To Anacreon in Heaven," a tune that had served any number of sets of verses over the years. Anacreon was a god who liked his wine and women, and drinking clubs sang to his good health.

"To Anacreon in Heaven" was written in the 1700s and was a popular song from the beginning. There were at least thirty versions of it before it was fitted with the words of the poem by Key called "In Defense of Fort McHenry." Anacreon lived a far from celibate life, so legend has it, and died at the age of eighty-five, having choked on a grape. Such is the inspiration for the country's first song. It was the constitutional song of the Anacreontic Society of London. John Stafford Smith, a proper Englishman, is the author of the work.

But for all of its popularity over the years since it was first published in Baltimore in the early part of the last century, "The Star Spangled Banner" was not designated the national anthem until President Woodrow Wilson did it in 1916. But even then, it took Congress until 1931 to pass an act that confirmed the designation.

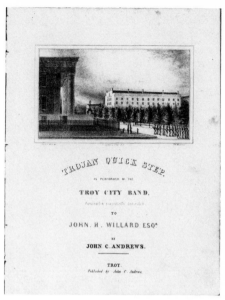

A lithography by the famous Currier. 1839.

A lithography by Currier for a Philadelphia publisher. 1839.

The Minstrel Period Begins

The next American music development was the minstrel period. And with some updating, the minstrel form is still with us, today. It began in the 1830s, or even earlier, and its high priest was Daddy Rice and his Jim Crow act.

The legend has entertainer Rice watching an old black beggar imitating a crow as he hopped and turned about singing this little ditty:

Wheel about, and turn about
an' do jis so;
Eb'ry time I wheel about,
I jump Jim Crow.

The Virginia Minstrels began in 1843 and were the first of the successful white minstrel groups. The Virginia group included Dan Emmett who was to score one of music's biggest successes when he wrote "Dixie." The minstrels needed a walk-around number — a song that could be sung while the minstrels moved

A popular minstrel tune, later known as "Turkey in the Straw." 1834

around the stage — and he came up with "Dixie."

The Christy Minstrels started a year later and they were the hottest attraction in show business for the next twenty years.

The tune that epitomized the period was "Old Zip Coon," later to sweep the country as "Turkey in the Straw," the staple of today's barn dance repertoire.

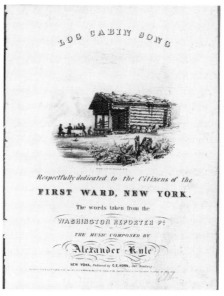

An early lithograph by Jenkins of New York. 1840.

The Stephen Foster Period

America's number one songwriter is unquestionably Stephen Foster. This deep-dyed Southerner from the magnolia-laden clime of Lawrenceville, Pennsylvania, touched the heart of America in a way that no one had before, or has since.

Foster only lived thirty-seven years, but in that brief span he gave birth to songs that will live as long as America.

And his profits were slight from his genius. From "Old Folks at Home" he

Some early ballads were dedicated to individuals. Circa 1850.

An innovative design of a Gottschalk tune. 1855.

Ground," $1,000. From his great songs: "Oh, Susanna," "Old Uncle Ned" and "Camptown Races," he received nothing. A typical annual income for him in his heyday was about $1,000. Even allowing for lower living costs, his compensation was shockingly low.

"Old Folks at Home" was published by Firth and Pond and had a success from the start. The publisher told the newspapers that he kept two presses on the job, added a third, and still couldn't keep up with the demand. Sales reached 40,000 in the first few weeks and, he said, would reach 100,000. Of course, they went far beyond that.

To put the success in perspective, realize that, today, fully one-half of all sheet music proves to be a failure. Three thousand copies of an instrumental and 5,000 of a song is considered to be a great sale.

In the very beginning, Foster was not proud of his role as a songwriter and

An early period Foster song that didn't last. 1850.

realized royalties of $1,647; from "My Old Kentucky Home," $1,372; from "Old Dog Tray," $1,080; and from "Massa's in de Col' Col'

8

even kept his name off "Old Folks at Home." He let E.P. Christy of Christy Minstrels put his name on the music because he didn't want to be associated with what were known as "Ethiopian melodies." A later version, however, did show Foster as the rightful composer.

In 1844 Foster had his first tune published, "Open thy Lattice, Love." It was published by Geo. P. Willig of Philadelphia. Foster was about eighteen at the time.

Contrary to Hollywood, Foster did not die in an alcoholic fog, brought on by disappointment. He was separated from his wife, it is true, and went to New York, it is true, and drank a good amount, it is true, but his cause of death was from a rent jugular, not a bottle of bourbon. While shaving in a garret in Manhattan, Foster, weak from work and from hunger, fainted. His head fell on a ceramic shaving bowl, breaking it, and the resulting jagged edge cut his

Foster wrote it, but didn't want his name on the music at first. 1852.

throat. He bled to death on the floor of his room. In his pocket was an envelope with the words, "Dear Hearts and Gentle People." It might have been Foster's greatest song, but that is all that historians know. Tin Pan Alley, of course, picked it up and used it as a tune, as in "Those dear hearts and gentle people who live and love in my home town."

Foster's most fragile and haunting "Beautiful Dreamer" was published after his death.

The Civil War Period

When the War Between the States broke out in 1861, the songwriters were ready. Pianos were well ensconced in parlors by that time—Jonas Chickering had established America's first piano factory some forty years earlier—and all of the songwriting ingredients were in place. The ingredients were, and still are: heroism, loss of loved ones, griev-

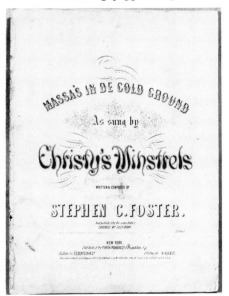

A popular Foster song that sold for twenty-five cents. 1852.

ing mothers, wives and children, and men returning from battle. It has been ever thus, even since the days of Homer.

Foster was to miss the great conflict and historians can only imagine what inspiring music he might have written. He died just as the battle lines were forming for the war's finale.

Two men came forward to establish themselves as the civil war writers: George F. Root and Henry C. Work.

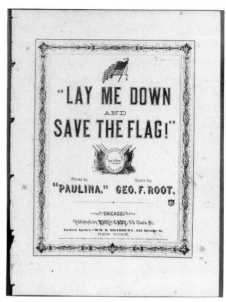

A patriotic song dedicated to the hero, Mulligan. 1864.

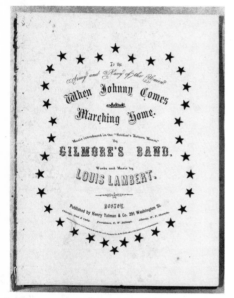

A Union song for the War Between the States. 1863.

Root wrote "Battle Cry of Freedom" and "Tramp, Tramp, Tramp," while Work wrote "Marching Through Georgia."

The Civil War period presents an uneven pattern for collectors. The Library of Congress lists show that there were 193 songs from the North and only 84 from the South. And, the southern songs, one might conclude, were printed on inferior paper and have not weathered as well as their northern counterparts.

In addition to the famous songs, such

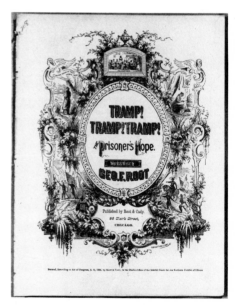

This cover art shows other tunes in the Root stable. 1864.

as "Tramp, Tramp, Tramp" and "Marching Through Georgia," the period produced: "John Brown's Body,"

"Maryland, my Maryland," "The Vacant Chair," "The Bonnie Blue Flag," "We Are Coming Father Abraham," "Just Before the Battle, Mother," "When Johnny Comes Marching Home," "All Quiet Along the Potomac Tonight," and "Tenting on the Old Camp Ground."

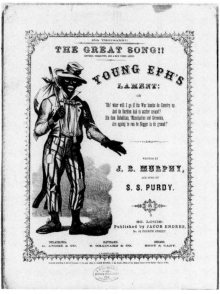

Negro dialect song that boasted of a 15,000-copy sale. 1863.

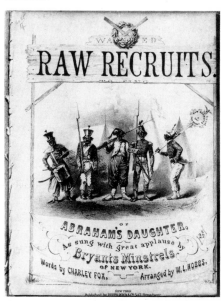

A minstrel favorite which sold for twenty-five cents. 1862.

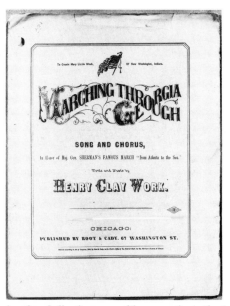

Another dedication song, this one to the author's cousin. 1865.

A ballad that presented its lyrics on the cover. 1864.

Patriotic figures have always been the subject of sheet music. 1859.

Lyrics were "Poetry" then and music sold for thirty cents "plain" and fifty cents in "color." 1860.

Buffalo and other cities in the East published music, along with Boston and New York. 1855.

The Romantic Period, 1870 to 1890

The Civil War was over, the wounds had been somewhat bound, and America began to settle down to peace and prosperity and "Manifest Destiny."

Sentiment and hearts and flowers were the guiding moods, and, as always, songwriters found a musical outlet for whatever mood was prevailing.

In those halcyon days, the parlor was the palace and, in it, the piano was the throne. Here, nightly, genteel young ladies, their families, and swains, would gather while the lady of the house played and others sang. Barbershop quartet singing began in this setting.

The songs were dripping with sentiment. "Silver Threads Among the Gold," (1873) sold more than two million copies. Other songs that echoed among the golden oak and antimicassars were:

"Darling Nellie Gray" (1856), "When You and I Were Young, Maggie." (1866), "Sweet Genevieve" (1869), "Grandfather's Clock" (1876), "A Flower from Mother's Grave" (1878), and "Why Did They Dig My Mother's Grave So Deep" (1880).

The sentimental ballad is old and basic. The first was in the Revolutionary War and was called "The Bank of the Dee" by John Tait (lyrics) and used the tune of the Irish air, "Langolee." The ballad flourished in the 1830s with Henry Russell from England and his "The Old Arm Chair" and "Woodman, Spare That Tree."

"Aura Lee" has come back with a vengeance more than 100 years later in the form of "Love Me Tender" by Elvis Presley. It sold more than a million copies in each of its lives.

The Golden Age of Sheet Music, the Gay Nineties

Song publishing began to take on the shape we know, today, in the 1890s with the emergence of Charles K. Harris as a songwriter and promoter *extraordinaire*. He came out of Milwaukee, Wisconsin, where his office door had the simple legend, "Songs Written to Order."

This was the period when Will Rossiter was going door-to-door to demonstrate his songs at department store counters. Joseph Stern and E. B. Marks were plugging their wares in beer halls with singing waiters and so-called water boys who weren't hired to haul water for thirsty patrons, but, rather, to suddenly bellow out a plug tune when its publisher hove into view.

Union Square in New York was coming to be the entertainment capital of the country and around it grew the music publishing industry. It would soon be succeeded by Forty-second Street and Broadway.

The taste of the time was saccharine; in art, in books and in music. "Take Back Your Gold," "She's More to Be Pitied Than Censured" were the songs sung around the ladies' parlor pianos.

Into this came Charles Harris who, barely out of his teens, wrote the song that started the big sale period with his five-million-seller, "After the Ball." It swept the country, and it started many who saw music as a kind of avocation to think of it as a means of getting rich, quick. Tin Pan Alley got a fast infusion and the popular music business was on its way.

Before, songwriters might sell their work for ten or fifteen dollars. Now, lyricists and composers started their own publishing firms and filled the nooks and crannies of Twenty-eight Street in New York. Songwriting had become a business as the century changed.

The legacy that the Gay Nineties left is still evident in much of our songwriting themes. In the litany, there are some basic stereotypes. Father is almost always an unromantic figure while motherhood is holy. Fatherhood was in some ways not unlike the present-day TV version of the male figure, a few steps above a gibbering idiot. As Isaac Goldberg said, there was " . . . just no profit in fathers" for songwriters of that day.

America Starts to Dance

The period from 1893 to 1898 was critical in popular music history in the United States because it was the time when the country was moving away from 3/4 time, or the waltz, to the 4/4 time of the sentimental ballad, the forerunner of the pop tune. The insistent rhythmic patterns of the minstrels and now the syncopation of ragtime moved the meter to a faster, more pronounced beat, one that made people want to get up and dance, dance, dance.

Fox trots were danced to this music with a cover by Matuick. 1927.

Ben Harney was a factor in this move with his "Ragtime Instructor" (1897), a piece of sheet music that sold phenomenally well and which helped the young bloods of the day understand what this dancing craze was all about.

And ragtime came to be a big factor in the advancement of sheet music sales— as all dance fads have been down through the years. Irving Berlin hit the wave at its crest with his "Alexander's Ragtime Band" which was not strictly a ragtime number, but what the heck! It was peppy and that was the thing.

The dance craze hit America running, just as the new century dawned in 1900. "The Turkey Trot" was a big favorite and it kicked off a host of imitations. The dance team of Vernon and Irene Castle propelled a lot of Americans to the dance floor in emulation and also sold a lot of sheet music along the way.

And the dance steps came out in endless number from Tin Pan Alley's seemingly inexhaustible cornucopia. There was the Grizzly Bear, The Maxixe, The Shimmy, The Shake, The Castle Walk and The Cake Walk. The Fox Trot came back for more and the Tango took center stage and held it when Rudolph Valentino gave it second life.

When the twenties started roaring, there were plenty of dance steps. The collegiate craze took over, helped by Hollywood. Tunes and steps like "The Varsity Drag" and "Collegiate" were part of the John Held flapper era.

Eva Tanguay sold a lot of music in her time. 1907.

14

Dance crazes kept coming through the thirties and forties with the Shag, Peckin', Truckin', Lambeth Walk, Jitterbug, Big Apple and so on and on, each with its own sheet music, and thus each with its own contribution to the total sales of what would have otherwise been a moribund market in the lean years after Wall Street laid an egg in 1929.

Frew was the artist on this typical cover for Irving Berlin. 1911.

All About Tin Pan Alley

Tin Pan Alley has come to be both a place and an idea. The place is easy, that was Twenty-eighth Street off Broadway in New York City and the time was in the late 1890s going on into the 1920s.

The idea is a bit more elusive but it has come to mean the epitome of American popular music, both the highs and the lows of the business. The highs, because from it came the most singable melodies the world has ever known, to the lows, the pandering to the basest of American tastes with nonsense songs and romantic drivel.

How did it begin? Music publishers stayed close to the musical theater at the turn of the century because it was that stage that presented their songs and it was that audience that bought their music in the department stores on Fourteenth Street and the other New York thoroughfares.

When the musical epicenter was on Union Square, one enterprising publisher moved to Twenty-eighth Street and another followed and another, and soon the block became a warren of small offices bristling with piano players and composers and publishers. If there was a garment district, and a financial district, then there had to be a music district, and Twenty-eighth Street was it.

Where did the name come from? Popular legend has it that Maurice Rosenfeld, a feature writer for the *New York World*, was in publisher Harry Von Tilzer's office one day when they heard the pingy sounds given from a piano being played with paper laid on the strings. This was done because secretive publishers were afraid that some of their new songs would be swiped by rival publishers as they were tested on the small pianos in their offices. The paper mute kept the sounds discretely within their own cubicle. Rosenfeld, who was on the street to do a story on the music publishers said when he walked down a corridor and heard the sounds, "Why, that sounds like a veritable Tin Pan Alley." He used the expression in his story for the paper and, in 1903, Tin Pan Alley had been named.

But Tin Pan Alley was a movable feast and just as it had moved uptown from the Union Square area to Twenty-eighth Street, it went farther uptown, to the Forty-second Street area — the new home of the musical stage — and even farther north to the Fifties to the Brill Building and to Rockefeller Center.

The relationship between the publisher and the musical stage was not merely a sentimental one. The publishers often paid for the scenery, and as the new shows were mounted, they arranged for the performers to plug their tunes. Placing a song with someone like Bert Williams or Anna Held or Nora Bayes meant a sure success with orders pouring in from all the cities on the route of the show when it left New York for tour.

In 1903, just as Monroe Rosenfeld was naming it, Tin Pan Alley, began its slow disintegration when one of the major firms, Witmark, moved uptown to Thirty-seventh Street. It was the beginning of the move that didn't stop until the Alley was a mere memory, about the time of World War I. Irving Berlin had moved up to Broadway and the trend was clear.

Where is Tin Pan Alley today? In many places. The Brill Building on New York's Broadway and Radio City's great complex have some 1,000 publishers. The Loop in Chicago has a few hundred and at Hollywood and Vine there are another several hundred. Nashville has a goodly amount of country publishers and Philadelphia and Boston are still home to some music publishers.

But Tin Pan Alley will not die, the National Music Council has seen to that. As part of the Bicentennial Program, a plaque was placed in the wall of the Chemical Bank Branch building at 36 West Twenty-eighth Street in the summer of 1976. The plaque testified to the fact that one time, not too long ago,

American popular music reached its zenith on this very street. There had been, indeed, a Camelot.

But the Alley lives on in a more tangible way, thanks to the new Songwriters' Hall of Fame. It's located, sadly enough, not on the old original Twenty-eighth Street location but, more appropriately for today's music world, in the heart of the Times Square entertainment district in New York. The address is One Times Square, between Forty-second and Forty-third Streets.

The Hall takes up an entire floor and is filled with memorabilia from America's songwriters. It boasts a small library, a research room, and a recording room where songwriters may go and reminisce for the benefit for a tape recorder — and posterity.

The idea came from three men: Howard Richmond, a publisher; songwriter Abe Olman, and the late lyricist, Johnny Mercer. They founded that Hall in 1968, but weren't able to get it

World War I melodies were not all grim — a Barbelle cover. 1916.

16

off the ground with a permanent home until January, 1977. Before moving to the Times Square location, the museum was housed in the offices of Richmond.

The admission to the Hall of Fame is set by the Hall's directors with the advice and consent of the National Academy of Popular Music. There are presently 164 members. Irving Berlin and Richard Rodgers were among the first inductees.

The Hall boasts the piano on which Fats Waller wrote "Honeysuckle Rose"; the typewriter Mercer used in writing "Lazybones," "I'm an Old Cowhand" and others; Victor Herbert's writing desk; an alligator-hide cigarette case given to Dorothy Fields by Cole Porter and, of course, hundreds of pieces of sheet music, letters, and photographs of the men and women who made Tin Pan Alley what it was and still is.

Admission to the Hall is free but one cannot just walk in. Visitors must telephone (212) 221-1252, beforehand. The museum is on the eighth floor of the building and is open from 11:00 A.M. to 3:00 P.M.

The Sheet Music Scene Today

The piano in the parlor has been replaced by the guitar in the basement, and that means that the children of today are not taking their songs in the same way.

Another aspect is that the explosion of music since the 1950s has meant that our youth are much more knowledgeable and are hearing so much music that they don't have to have the music written out and in front of them the way they might have had several decades ago.

Another factor is that the new music today is not written down, so much of it is improvised, working more with chords than with strict, always-the-same melody lines.

Young musicians today write their own music, and most rock bands have their own repertoire and books and, with some notable exceptions, they only exist as manuscripts and notes toward manuscripts.

They have memorized the tunes, self-written, or otherwise. When was the last time anyone saw a young band reading from music? Orchestras of forty years ago had standard repertoire that included the Hit Parade — what is the Hit Parade today? — and you could count on bands from Boston to Oakland playing not only the same tunes, say "September in the Rain" and "Three Little Fishies," but playing the same orchestration purchased in music stores 3,000 miles apart.

Hazel Meyer points out that today, music publishers have lost their dignity along with their control of the music business. Where once they selected, groomed, and published songs winnowed from professional sources, they are now in the ignominious position of acting as go-betweens, scrambling like fiddler crabs to collect anything at all that the recording companies will accept.

"The richly catalogued, old independent firms are disenchanted. Disgusted with these crazy sounds and faced with the futility of trying to interest A and R men in their sedate copyrights, they are resigned to sitting it out until sanity and melody return to popular music. Meanwhile, they continue in business on the bountiful harvest of royalties forthcoming from ASCAP for their hundreds of standard ballads; favorites even the new discordant sounds cannot drown out," she points out.

The Copyright Situation

With the date of sheet music publication such an important factor for collectors, it makes sense to review some of America's copyright history.

Prior to 1831, music was not mentioned in the copyright protection laws, even though there had been a copyright procedure dating back to 1790. There was no copyright law before then because there wasn't a country. England worried about copyrights and about hanging on to her new colonies on the American continent.

In 1909, the Congress passed the basic copyright law that was to last until 1976 when its successor was passed. The 1909 law permitted copyrights to last for twenty-eight years and then allowed for one renewal of twenty-eight years. After that, the music went into the public domain and it was every man for himself. The authors and composers pointed out that it was possible for someone to write a piece of music at, say, age twenty, copyright once, and then again, and have the copyright run out while the composer was seventy-six, listening to his music being played and sold without as much as a penny coming to him.

The new law grants copyright protection for the author's life, plus fifty years after, so that his estate will benefit for those years after his death.

The Sunday Supplements

Music publishers, during the late 1890s and the first ten years of this century, were faced with a condition that was hard to cope with. They were forced to permit songs to be reproduced in their entirety in the supplements of the large Sunday newspapers. This really meant giving away a piece of fifty-cent music—the typical price of the day—for nothing. When they wanted a song from a theatrical or musical production, they would strike at the music publisher through the medium of the theatrical producer by holding out the bait of a one- or two-page spread of press matter with pictures, advertising the show in which the number was sung.

Newspaper readers often got a bonus of sheet music with their Sunday edition. 1903.

That caused some consternation, understandably, along Tin Pan Alley. After all, they could argue with some justification, they had put their hard-earned money into finding a song, promoting it, and then trying to sell it to the public for fifty cents, or more. But now, that prized sheet music with its glossy, colored cover was found free on Sunday morning, nestled next to the comic section in the Sunday paper. The copyright law of the time, this was before 1909, permitted the practice, and with the interest in popular music at a high point in that period, "Why not?" said the publisher. The newspaper had some clout to use to persuade the publisher to grant permission to print the music.

There are still many copies of this kind of sheet music around, but they are extremely fragile since they were made of newsprint and were intended for a more temporary use than the regular sheet music which was printed on good quality, coated stock and designed for a much longer life span.

A good example—of the hundreds that were printed—is "My Ruby Belle" from the *New York Jounal-American* of April 3, 1904.

CHAPTER III

The Song Plugger at his Trade

In Douglas Gilbert's *Lost Chords*, he points out that in the 1860s, printed music was still not common, but the words of songs in penny ballad form were hawked by old men and women on the streets of the cities. The touts would fasten the music to a rack and, as the potential customer approached, they would hum or sing the melody of the tune. Singing on the streets was a common occurence in that period, and the hawkers tried to get their songs wafted into the air to be picked up and sung by passersby, motormen on trolleys, or cyclists.

These hawkers, for they truly "hawked their wares," persisted well into the 1880s in New York, but they took a somewhat sinister turn as the century ended. Michael Cregansteine, known as the "King of the Song Sheet Men," cornered the business and trained his men from his quarters in New York City's Bowery. Cregansteine paid his suppliers forty cents per hundred for the song sheets and his hawkers sold them in turn for one to five cents each, a tidy profit.

Everybody knew songs in those days. A good song, Gilbert points out, lived for years instead of being murdered by overexposure in a matter of a few weeks. At the home, the families would gather about the piano, and accompanied by a flute, or guitar or accordian, the young people would fill in the evenings with a popular ballad. Sheet music was essential, else how would they know how the tune went?

But it was song plugging, the art of selling the song, that made American popular music different from all other music of all other countries. It was the

year of the American spirit, and on all sides Americans were bursting their buttons with inventions and devices and new frontiers. The world was their oyster; after all, weren't they Americans?

So the popular song got the treatment of the salesman, and the music business has never been the same since.

The inventiveness of the song plugger beggars description, even in this age of the supersalesman. Here are a few ways in which the plugger carried out his trade:

* In a bar, waiters would circulate among the tables singing plug songs from the publishers. They were slipped silver dollars for the evening's work; good pay in those days. Irving Berlin began his career as a singing waiter as a place called Nigger Mike's in New York where he would warble the plug songs of the day in his reedy, almost falsetto, tones.

* Talent scouts would haunt the Lower East Side synagogues on church days and check out the young boy cantors, singing their Kol Nidres, and afterward offer them more silver dollars to sing their songs in the department stores and theatres where plugging was a matter of life.

The hard-eyed pluggers felt that the young Jewish singers had a schmaltzy, or chicken fat, style that was just right for the saccharine ballads of the day.

* At department stores, the plugging reached a high commercial level as pluggers would hand out chorus slips of the ubiquitous song as the other plugger manned the piano and played the tune. On Saturday afternoons a song would sell 1,000 copies under this

20

barrage.

* Was there a six-day bike race in town at Madison Square Garden? The song plugger would be there, moving through the crowds, singing his song, and handing out the always present song sheets, or chorus slips. Was there a political rally? Then there too would be the song plugger, hawking and singing his wares. Any gathering place was an occasion, a platform for the song plugger.

The logical extension of all this plugging was the song slide. That was the work of George H. Thomas who, in 1892, went to work on a tune called "The Little Lost Child" and, using real policemen with some friends and an actor or two, made a series of pictures that illustrated the heartrending story of a child lost in the great city. As the slides flashed on the screen, the plugger would sing the tune and the audience would start to sing along.

De Witt C. Wheeler produced slides for the Witmark's Herman A Rosenberg, beginning in 1911, as the Greater New York Slide Co. The Noon Club under Harry Blair at Shapiro, Bernstein was doing slides in the 1930s.

For all this catch-as-catch-can method of plugging a song, it fell inevitably to the master promoter in America—the advertising man—to get into the act. He did, just after the turn of the century, and fell on his face. The promotion of sheet music defied all of the persuasion of the advertising man.

Harry Link took Berlin's "Smile and Show Your Dimple" (later reborn in a more successful version as '"Easter Parade"). He used Philadelphia as a test market and promoted the song with ads in the newspaper, on billboards, and used other techniques adored by admen of the period. It flopped. The music sold 2,500 copies in the whole campaign and a department store could sell that many copies of a hit tune in an afternoon on New York's Fourteenth Street.

On plugging, E.B. Marks has a poignant recollection: "The best songs came from the gutter in those days. Indeed, when I started publishing in 1894 there was no surer way of starting a song off to popularity than to get it sung as loudly as possible in the city's lowest dives. If a publisher knew his business, he always launched a sales campaign by impressing his song on the happily befogged consciousness of the gang in the saloons and beer halls. When a number was introduced from the stage of one of the more pretentious beer halls, that was a plug."

Mark and his partner Joseph Stern used to cover sixty beer joints a week pushing their wares. They would pass out chorus slips to tables and then get soloists to sing the songs from the stage, or from the busboy post, or wherever they could. The best thing was to get the audience to sing along.

In the history of publishers who were also pluggers, Will Rossiter is significant. He was the first to sing his own songs in retail stores and also the first to issue cheap songbooks. He was the one who began the practice—later carried to a high art—of adorning the sheet music cover with colorful artwork.

CHAPTER IV

Some All-time Best Sellers

Song publishers play roulette, hoping that they'll get a big score from one song, enough sales from a smash hit to make up for all of the mediocre sellers that take time and money and produce little profit.

They sometimes make it, but more often, they fall far short. Over the years there has developed a kind of all-time hit parade. Publishers tend to inflate sales figures, and these figures are all supplied by publishers so should be considered as *caveat lector,* but they do represent a fair list of the jumbo sheet music sellers of all time:

This best seller is still popular. 1909.

"The End of a Perfect Day" (1910). 5,000,000
"Down by the Old Mill Stream" (1909) 5,000,000
"Let Me Call You Sweetheart" (1900) 5,000,000
"After the Ball"(1892). 5,000,000
"Meet Me Tonight in Dreamland" (1909). 5,000,000
"Till We Meet Again"(1918) 3,500,000
"Over There"(1917) 3,000,000
"School Days"(1907) 3,000,000
"I'm Forever Blowing Bubbles"(1919). 2,600,000
"Joan of Arc"(1916). 2,000,000
"Ramona"(1927). 2,000,000
"Silver Threads Among the Gold"(1873). 2,000,000

The more-than-one-million sheet music sellers include "Dinah" (1925), "Carolina Moon" (1928), "Pagan Love Song" (1929), "My Blue Heaven" (1927), "The Wedding of the Painted Doll" (1929), "Sonny Boy" (1928), "Among My Souvenirs" (1927), "Smiles" (1917), "There's a Rainbow 'Round My Should-er" (1928), and "Wait Till the Sun Shines Nellie" (1905).

One of the very few songs to sell more than one million copies of sheet music since the heyday of music publishing is Irving Berlin's "White Christmas," published in 1942. Bing Crosby's phenomenally successful recording had a stimulating effect upon the sheet music.

But this list is not complete. There have been other jumbo sellers over the years; these are the ones that have stayed with us as permanent items in our popular music heritage.

CHAPTER V

The Black in American Popular Music

The first songs about the Negro were serious and melancholy. Two early examples were "The Desponding Negro" by William Reeve in 1793 and "Poor Black Boy" in 1794.

As the Century wore on, the Negro became a key actor in American song. Daddy Rice started the "Jump Jim Crow" and the "Coal Black Rose" was popular when it came out in 1827. "Old Zip Coon" was published, then changed its title and became "Turkey in the Straw."

One early tune was "Jim Brown" in 1835. It had for its title page "A Celebrated Nigger Song." "Jim Along Josey" was first sung in 1838 in the play, *The Free Nigger of New York.*

But why the Negro, anyway? Why was he such an important figure in sheet music and the sweep of popular songs in America? Isaac Goldberg in Tin Pan Alley says that the Negro is the symbol of our uninhibited expression, of our uninhibited action. "He is our catharsis. He is the disguise behind which we may, for a releasing moment, regain that part of ourselves which we have sacrificed to civilization. He helps us to a double deliverance. What we dare not say, often, we freely sing. Music, too, is an absolution, and what we would dare not sing in our own plain speech we freely sing in the Negro dialect, or in terms of the black. The popular song, like an unseen Cyrano, provides love speeches for that speechless Christian,

the public. And the Negro, a black Cyrano, adds lust to the passion."

The coon songs, and that's what they were called on the sheet music itself, hit from the 1890s through the first World War. Most of them were written by whites who, in the best minstrel tradition, perpetuated the sterotype of the Negro as a shiftless, amoral, watermelon-eating darky. It was a time, too, when there were Dutch comedy acts which mocked the Germans and Irish comedy acts which mocked the Irish among us. Vaudeville owes a great deal to the Jewish comedians who exaggerated their ethnic traits to convulsed audiences. And the comedy of the stage found its counterpart in the music. They're all there, but the music, again, only reflects and does not lead, national culture and mores.

One interesting reaction to the coon songs came from a top writer of the period, Kerry Mills, or F.A. Mills. Mills, a white man, was incensed at the coon song written by black vaudevillian Ernest Hogan, "All Coons Look Alike to Me." He sat down and wrote a tune that, while it is hardly on the lips of millions of Americans today, has been embraced by traditional jazz bands: "At a Georgia Camp Meeting." In the song, Mills lends some dignity to the black in his revels and, for the first time, invests the black with some style and grace.

CHAPTER VI

The Business Side of the Music

Music, in America, is big business. It was big business back in the latter half of the nineteenth century when the piano moved into the parlor, with sheet music following on its heels. It stayed that way during the romantic period and the golden period, and then when mechanical reproduction began in the early teens, through the phonograph record and the movies, it caught fire.

It's a big ticket item by any reckoning. Shemel and Krasilovsky in their *This Business of Music* report that the number of persons who played musical instruments in 1970 was 31.5 million. The average American in that year was listening to 17.5 hours of radio programs per week. And Americans were spending more for high fidelity and concert music recordings than they were for all spectator sports combined. On Super Bowl Sunday that may be hard to believe, but it's true.

The public has now an investment in more than 300 million radio sets and 85 million TV sets. More than 80 percent of our homes, the ones that have electricity, have record players. Over 57 million phonographs are in use and of these, 80 percent are stereo. There are 12 million eight-track players on hand and that many cassettes. The annual sales of musical instruments, accessories and printed music has gone over the one-billion-dollar mark.

Collections by performing rights organizations have gone up, too. In 1970 ASCAP took in $72.5 million on behalf of its 12,600 writers, composers and publishers compared to the 1963 take of $38 million. BMI took in $34 million compared to the $15 million in

1963. SESAC took in $32 million for 200 publishers representing 375 catalogs.

Although the sale of printed music, including sheet music, has now become a small part of the industry, there is still some activity in the area of music for guitars and electronic organs.

Bromo Seltzer was one of many firms that used sheet music to help sales. Circa 1885.

Records continue to flourish. There are about 6,000 singles and 4,000 albums released each year. Of this torrent of sound, not a great deal reaches the public ear. Little more than 29 percent of the songs are played once by disc jockeys over the air and more than 59 percent are never played at all. That's for singles. For albums, 70 percent are played more than once and less than 20 percent are never played at all.

Sales of single sheet music in the United States have slowed to a mere trickle. In 1910, a typical year, and by no means the zenith, the total sales of popular songs in sheet music form reached $2 billion. From 1902 to 1907, about 100 different songs had reached a sales level of more than 100,000 while 40 had gone over 200,000. Some 30 had gone beyond 250,000. Four had been jumbo sellers with Williams and Van Alstyne's "In the Shade of the Old Apple Tree" topping out at 700,000.

The market for sheet music got active in the 1880s and 1890s when department stores throughout the country began to have counters for it. The Sunday newspaper supplements in the 1890s department stores were printing songs to distribute as advertising. And, of course, some of the best collectors' items, today, are the ones that were used as advertising for the Studebaker Company, the Great Northern Railroad, the Bromo Seltzer Company, and many more. In the 1880s, a hit song might sell 50,000 copies. Just ten years later a sale of less than 250,000 was not regarded highly when some were hitting the one million mark. "After the Ball" was the first to go over one million.

The price of sheet music has varied all over the lot. Surprisingly, the cost was relatively high when the romantic period began and stayed high through the golden period and until after World War II when they started to tumble. Music cost about sixty cents in the latter part of the nineteenth century, and this was at a time when sixty cents was three meals in decent restaurants, or a hat, or a pair of gloves, or several dozen pullets. It dipped to fifty; or occasionally forty cents, as the century turned, but it stayed relatively high. And yet this was the time when sheet music had its biggest sales. Interestingly, when the retail price for music was sixty cents,

the publisher was only getting twenty-three cents. Talk about markup!

Price wars began in music, too. Woolworth's Five and Ten sold it for a dime and these prices spurred the one-million sales figures and World War II. The old-line publishers resisted the lowering of price because they felt that once people were used to paying a dime, they would never again pay the forty cents that had been the going price in "the good old days."

In the first, early days of Tin Pan Alley, songs were sold for forty cents. By the early 1900s, the price had come down to twenty-five cents. The jobbers were charged about 50 percent of the retail figure and the publishers paid royalties of five cents per copy. The royalty in turn is split between the composer and author. In 1916, sheet music was selling for as low as ten cents, spurred by Woolworth, with royalty reduced to one cent. Since that time the price has tended to rise and the average price in 1930 was thirty cents per copy. Some still believe that increase from ten cents was a marketing error and it was that, rather than movies and radio that killed sheet music.

But today, the price doesn't seem to matter that much. Some hit songs of recent vintage such as "Love is Blue" can still sell in excess of one million copies in the first year, but that is unusual.

Typically, the songwriter's contract calls for three to five cents per copy of sheet music sold plus 50 percent of the royalties of sales abroad. Under the usual formula the minimum payment is either a straight royalty of three cents per copy or a sliding scale which starts at two and one-half cents per copy for the first 100,000 and then goes up to five cents for sales of more than 500,000.

E. B. Marks recalled that in about 1922 the radio craze began. He said that when radio moved to the forefront, songs were made in a week and killed off in sixty days. "The public hears so many songs that it has long since ceased to distinguish between them." Before a person can decide to buy a piece of sheet music it is succeeded in the hearer's ears by six other songs, Marks complained. A song that sold 100,000 in the mid-twenties was a big hit. "More songs are produced than ever before," he wrote, "but nobody profits from them except the broadcasters."

When World War I ended it was clear that sheet music was no longer the mainstay of music business. The industry had disdained the two cents per side that had been paid by the record companies, but it became significant as single record sales soared.

Alexander Woolcott did a study of Irving Berlin, and some of his findings shed light on the relative ranking of the various forms of music reproduction in the twenties and thirties. He took four Berlin tunes and compared their sales in four forms:

* $15 for the basic piano arrangement.
* $20 for the plates for the regular sheet music printing.
* $17 for printing 2,000 professional copies to be sent to singers, orchestra leaders, etc.
* $25 for vocal arrangements.
* $40 for 500 copies of the arrangements.
* $75 to $150 for an arranger to make a dance band orchestration.
* $1 per page for the dance band orchestrations.
* $90 for 5,000 copies of the regular sheet music for distribution to jobbers, etc.
* $250 for promotional mailing of regular sheet music to orchestra leaders, singers, etc.
* $25 for the cost of the title page drawing, or artwork.

Clearly, the hard-eyed publishers of that day didn't have much money left over for a Picasso or Stuart Davis to do their covers. Twenty-five dollars may have been on the low side, but in the lean days of the thirties, artists worked for what they could get.

The markup for the retail outlet was 40 percent. Thus, a thirty-five cent

Title	Duration of Sales	Sheet	Piano Rolls	Phono Records
"You'd Be Surprised"	50 weeks	783,982	145,505	888,790
"Say It with Music"	75 weeks	374,408	102,127	1,239,050
"Nobody Knows"	70 weeks	1,143,690	62,204	843,062
"All by Myself"	75 weeks	1,053,493	161,650	1,225,083

What It Costs to Get It Published

Robert Bruce's *So You Want to Write a Song* (Mayfair, 1935) gives a good breakdown of the costs attendant to publishing a piece of popular sheet music in the mid-thirties. When the publisher—in those depression years—set out to bring a tune to the public, here's what he was facing:

piece of sheet music netted the publisher only twenty-one cents and then he had to pay the composers and his overhead.

With these costs, publishers were fortunate to be able to publish more than four tunes a month. The typical cost to publish in the mid-thirties was $1,000 per tune. The margins were slim, indeed.

27

CHAPTER VII

Notes from a Music Researcher's Files

Much sheet music between the 1880s and up to the middle of the 1930s was inspired by dramatic events, taken right from the newspaper's front pages. There were songs about floods, famines, and wars. There were songs about people trapped in caves in Kentucky and about the sinking of the *Lusitania.*

Charles Lindberg flew solo to Paris and more than a 100 songs followed in his prop wash. Harry Thaw was put in the slammer for shooting architect Stanford White and there was a song for him.

In those days of less communication clutter, people who wanted to remember the event would buy music and put it away, with no idea at all of ever playing it. Many didn't even have pianos, but the purchase of the sheet music, like keeping the front page of the local paper the day of your first child is born, was a way of keeping the date, or the event, very much in your mind, a keepsake in song.

The fast growth of records, and the equally fast drop of sheet music sales can be seen by a look at the figures for 1954 when the LP records were in full bloom. Gross receipts from sheet music were $12 million while records grossed $85 million. That year greeting cards did $25 million and books, $665 million.

America is a whistling and humming and singing nation. It is also a songwriting nation. The Library of Congress has somewhat more than three million different pieces of sheet music in their files, all written by Americans from the time of the Plymouth Colony to yesterday.

But that's just the pieces that were good enough to be published. The Copyright Office reports that in the most recent five-year span, almost 500,000 individual songs were filed by Americans.

The Copyright Office began in 1790. That could mean, and the office couldn't estimate the number without a massive audit, that perhaps some seven to ten million songs have been written and sent to the Copyright Office for registration. That's a right smart of music!

Autographed sheet music covers are a collecting item, Klamkin reports. A copy of the "Pickwick Polka," written in honor of Charles Dickens's visit to the United States in 1867, and signed by him, is an important item. Another is the kind that has been signed by the composer, or the lyricist, or the performer.

Speaking of copyrights, aspiring songwriters should know — as collectors already do — that titles of songs cannot be copyrighted. That's why there are dozens of "I Love You"'s and "Do You Love Me"'s. If you want to title your next tune "Home, Sweet Home," there's nothing to stop you.

Surprisingly, one of the best places to buy music is England. The devaluation of the pound means dollars will go farther and there is a good supply of music in shops around London. Much of it is sold at one-third stateside levels. Pan Am's spacious 747s are the best way to go; they'll give you elbow room to sort out your music and they fly to London on frequent schedules.

CHAPTER VIII

The Sheet Music Itself

There's a knack to reading the sheet music, especially the cover, quite apart from the music itself. There's the title, of course, and the writers, or writer. If only one writer, it means that he, or she, wrote both the words and music. When there's a team, it might simply be a listing of several names as the authors or it will show "music" by one, and "lyrics," or words, by the other. If the song is from a movie, or a stage production, it will contain the name of the production, the producer, credits for choreography, and the writer of the book of the show. When the song is from a show, the cover will often have a list of a few other songs from the production.

The publisher is always shown on the cover with, more often than not, the address. Cover art can range from an art deco masterpiece of 1920s chic to

Early automobile travel inspired many popular tunes. 1914.

photographs of long-forgotten singers, or band leaders.

In the music covers before the 1930s, there will often be a large 5 or 6 or 3.5. This is simply a code to the dealer that the retail price should be fifty cents, or sixty cents, or thirty-five cents, and that he should figure his markup from that base.

Probably the most important piece of information for the collector or dealer, is the year of the copyright printed on practically all pieces of music from the early nineteenth century on. The date is, for all practical purposes, the date of publication of the song and is the dating device used by collectors. The copyright date is the year that the publisher, or whoever held the copyright, filed the song with the Copyright Office of the United States.

The date is almost always on the bottom of the first page of the music itself. Most tunes, from the 1880s on, use the Roman numberals; Arabic numbers were used before 1890.

If your high school Latin is a bit rusty, here are some quick translations:

M equals 1,000
C equals 100
V equals 5
L equals 50
D equals 500
X equals 10
I equals one

The music you will be looking at will be from the nineteenth and twentieth centuries. If it's from the eighteenth century, you're sitting on a goldmine.

You'll quickly discover the trick of putting together a roman numeral. If the music is published in a year in the 1900s, the first three letters will be MCM. A letter, or number, just before a letter with a larger value means that you subtract and add it to the first number in the set. Thus M is 1,000 and the C, or 100, subtracted from the second M makes it 900. This added to the first M (1,000) makes 1,900. After that's established, the next series will give the precise year. MCMXII, or 1912. MCMII, or 1902. Nineteenth century (that is, the 1800s) dates begin with MDCCC and then add numbers for the year. MDCCCLXIV is 1864. MDCCCV is 1805. Simple, isn't it?

Generally speaking, all sheet music is divided into two sizes. Before and during World War I it came in the large size, or 13½ inches by 10½ inches. After the War, about 1920, most songs were published in the standard size of today which is 9 inches by 12 inches. To save paper during World War I, there was a 10-by-7-inch version around, but there were not too many made in that smaller size. Those which are still available have become collectibles for sheet music fans.

Covers of music starting in the mid-thirties, or so, will occasionally show a miniature music staff of a bar or two with a series of notes. This is the indication to a singer of the actual range of the tune. If you are a basso profundo, there isn't much point in buying a tune that is in the upper register. Some music publishers would publish various arrangements of their tunes in a range of keys so that a mezzo-soprano

or a bathroom baritone could find his range.

In addition to the small music staff, the cover might simply say in the key of F or G or whatever, as another instruction to the performer buying the music.

Inside the Music: What the Song Is About

There has been so much emphasis on the cover of the sheet music and there have been so many subcollecting groups that splinter off in search of Barbelle covers or patriotic covers or Shirley Temple covers that the original reason for the music-in-the-first-place has been lost sight of: It's the notes on the paper that started the whole thing, and that's worthy of a closer look.

The rule of four is the one that guides most popular musical numbers. Typically, there will be an introduction of four measures, or bars, that will set the mood, the key and the tempo of the song. Then, again, typically but not always, there will be a verse which is a multiple of four, and could be eight or sixteen measures. That goes into the chorus which is often thirty-two bars. The chorus is the melody, the tune that is remembered, the part that America sings, whistles, or hums.

The rule of four applies to chorus as well. It usually is made up of stanzas of four eight-bar sections arranged, if you remember learning your poetry in high school English, of A-A-B-A refrains. Thus, the first two eight-bar sections are identical, give or take a note or two on the final eight; the next eight, or B strain, is completely different and is called the release, or bridge, because it takes you back to the final eight, which is identical to the first eight, or the A strain.

In reading the music, the top line, or staff, is marked with a treble clef and is the melody; it is shown in single notes for the singer to pick out the tune. The words are positioned precisely below.

The second line is also marked by a treble clef and indicates the notes and chords of the melody to be played by the right hand on the piano. The third line, marked by a bass, or F, clef contains the notes of rhythm and harmony that are to be played by the left hand.

The little symbols that look like boxes are the chord symbols and tell the ukulele player—when there is no piano in sight—where to place his fingers on the strings to make the appropriate chord to match the melody note. Sometimes the chord symbol is given, a G, or B♭ or C, or whatever is the appropriate chord.

Setting up the chord symbols is not a routine task and some of the better ones, like May Singhi Breen, were so much in demand that they got a credit line on the cover when they set up the chords.

Thus, the music provides words, melody line for both verse and chorus, and instructions for ukulele or guitar.

The verse is often the most interesting part of the song and was designed to introduce, or set the scene for the chorus, by telling the listener what the background of the song is all about. The chorus then came along to nail down the idea, hopefully indelibly on the consciousness of the listener.

Caring for and Displaying the Music

One characteristic of sheet music is that it is very fragile. Keeping and displaying it for others is worth the time and trouble. Perhaps the best way is to put the run-of-the-mill pieces in plastic bags that can be bought at any grocery store. The large size easily accommodates the largest music that you'll have—the 10 ½ inch by 13 ½ inch variety—and will leave plenty of room for your 9 inch by 12 inch sizes. You can handle them without damaging them and still be able to see the cover and read all of the pertinent information. Also, the slippery plastic jackets will allow faster shuffling when you're digging through the pile for an item.

Because it's so fragile, tears come easily but they can be repaired. Mending tape works fine but use the newer variety, Magic Tape, and not the old, transparent Scotch tape that tends to become rigid after some use and has a tendency to turn a bit yellow. Use it sparingly but firmly so as to keep tears from spreading.

Some of the older sheet music that's on the market these days has been pulled from a bound volume and it will show signs of battle. Many singers, and even some nonprofessionals, would have their sheet music bound into a book for convenience, never imagining that someday someone would want to pull it apart and sell the songs separately.

CHAPTER IX

The Art of the Cover

There is little doubt that the attraction of the cover of the sheet music is an appeal for many collectors. There is music inside, of course, but it could be pure Egyptian hieroglyphics as far as they are concerned because the cover is the thing.

There are two basic approaches to cover collecting. One is the celebrity or star approach, which is where people collect not "There's a Rainbow 'Round My Shoulder," but because it has a picture of Al Jolson on the cover. Or "The Good Ship Lollipop," not because of the intrinsic value of that slight tune, but because Shirley Temple is on the cover. In truth, this school is moved more by the person than by the music and collects stills from motion pictures or posters or other memorabilia featuring their favorites even as they collect sheet music.

Another school collects the artists, and there is a substrata of collecting that sees this approach as the ne plus ultra of sheet music collecting. Professional collectors in lists increasingly like to indicate that such and such sheet music features a cover by Barbelle or DeTakacs, or Pud Lane; all artists who did many covers over the years.

The giant in this area is E.T. Paull, a music publisher whose covers of fire engines rushing through the night, or gaudy parades or other heroic scenes are beautiful examples of American art and deserve a place in the American art gallery on their own merit. But the Paull covers are different from all the rest. Here is a rundown on some of the better known sheet music artists:

Starmer: His covers run from the late 1890s through World War II.

Albert Barbelle. Barbelle's style was more like that of a magazine illustrator with romantic-looking men and women in sophisticated table or pastoral settings.

Andre DeTakacs. He had many styles but the one that stands out is his cubist period best seen on "Pork and Beans."

Helen Westin in her book *Introducing the Song Sheet* has done a good amount of research into the cover artists. In addition to the three well-known ones, she has identified Pfeiffer, John Frew, Frederick S. Manning, Carter, Myers, Pryor, and someone known only as R.S.

Gene Buck, himself a lyricist and the onetime president of ASCAP, is also a cover artist and his name will appear on a number of tunes of the twenties, including "Everybody's Doin' it Now" and "General Grant's March." He designed for publisher Whitney and Warren and was one of the first to work in color. He designed some 5,000 pieces of art before he developed eye trouble and had to quit.

Pud Lane was another artist who came along in the late twenties and thirties and whose work adorns a period when the movies and Tin Pan Alley's more routine songs were being purveyed.

Starmer and Barbelle were certainly the two most typical of the artists of the period from 1900 through the twenties, the Golden Age of sheet music. They portrayed, as befitted the style and the mood of the music they were presenting, romantic and gauzy pictures of happy men and women looking adoringly at each other. DeTakacs was also of the same school, but he was more interested in the figures and made them more prominent, while Starmer and

Barbelle were more interested in the overall tableau. Here are some of the tunes they did cover art for:

Starmer:
  "Take Me to My Alabam'"
  "Flow Along River Tennesee"
  "Sweet Little Caribou"
  "At the End of the Road"
  "My Girl from the USA"
  "Sante Fe"
  "Indianola"
  "Golden Arrow"
  "Once Again"
  "Red Moon"
  "My Old Kentucky Home"
  "My Hawaiian Sunshine"
  "I Couldn't Believe My Eyes"
  "Roll On, Missouri"
  "Ypsilanti"
  "My Lotus Flower"
  "When I Waltz with You"
  "Moonlight Bay"
  "Goodnight, Dear Heart"
Barbelle:
  "When the Yanks Go Marching
    Home"
  "Who-oo? You-oo, That's Who-oo"
  "Huggable, Kissable You"
  "Where Rolls the Oregon"
  "For Me and My Gal"
  "Is She My Girl Friend"
  "All the Quakers Are Shoulder
    Shakers"
  "Huckleberry Finn"
  "Lonesome and Sorry"
  "Rain"
Pfeiffer:
  "On Ranch 101"
  "She Is the Sunshine of Virginia"
  "I'm Going Down to Tennessee"
  "Sit Down You're Rocking the Boat"
DeTakacs:
  "I'm Going to Fight My Way Right
    Back to Caroline"
  "Pride of the Prairie"

"Denver Town"
"Piney Ridge"
"I'm Always Chasing Rainbows"
"Blue Feather"
"Kerry Mills Barn Dance"
"In the Valley of the Moon"

Hollywood discovered football and sheet music in the twenties. 1929.

But there were others who signed their work during this period, and their work is somewhat more interesting for collectors in that it is a bit harder to find than the well-known cover artists. Some of this group includes:

Wohlman. "Lost (A Wonderful Girl)" in 1922. An interesting combination of graphic design and illustration. Also "Swanee River Rose" (1924) "Moody Moon", etc.

Perret. On his "You Know You Belong to Somebody Else" (1922), there is a beginning of art deco with clean, sharp lines and stylistic figure of a woman.

Hoffman. Some pretty poster art on

"Little Lost Rolling Stone" (1923).

Politzer. His work with illustration is better than average and shows well on "I Want to Borrow a Sweet Mama" in 1922. He also did "I'm Missing the Kissing of Someone" (1926), with a woman looking pensively at a picture on a table.

Matuick. "Gorgeous" (1927) shows a pretty girl in a windswept dress.

L.H. portrays a sweeping, dancing couple on "The Merry Widow Waltz" (1908), and Bittmar draws angels for the cover of "Angels of the Night" back in 1909.

B. Harris. An excellent art deco adherent, he did "Moon About Town" (1933) and "Dinner for One, Please James" (1935).

Jenkins. He was from an earlier period and did a classic design for "Silver Threads Among the Gold" in 1901.

Artist Politzer and flappers combined for this unusual cover. 1922.

Edgar Keller. His work was bold and expansive and had touches of art nouveau. His best work is on "Tessie" (1902) and "Winter" (1910).

J. Frew. "A Koon Kick" (1903), "Run Home and Tell Your Mother" (1911), and "California and You" (1914) are among his works. His work is so much like Barbelle, and Starmer, that at first glance it is hard to distinguish them.

Art deco was the rage when artist Leff did this cover. 1932.

Frederick S. Manning. His work tended to be more in the area of type design and graphic layout. One of his most typical is "I Couldn't Tell Them What to Do" in 1933. Kate Smith is on the cover with typical Manning design setting off the photograph.

Some of the best work, even that from the golden period of sheet music, is not signed. When the work is a dreary copy of the famous artists, that is one thing, but in the case of at least one cover, "Siboney" in 1929, it is a shame. The cover shows a pair of latin dancers in clear, hard lines and colorful costumes, in a sinuous pose while in the background, a humorous Cuban band plays merrily on. It is kind of poster art that is in the best tradition of Toulouse-Lautrec but no clue as to artist.

The trend of the cover art matched perfectly, stride for stride, the trends that were taking place in the music world and in the art world outside. The romantic drawings of the turn of the century began to give way in the twenties to a more modern art, or art deco, reflecting the changes of the real world. The emphasis began to be on design and color, not on the tableaux of the period before 1920. One of the best artists of this period was Leff whose work can be seen on "Rockin' on the Porch" (1934), "Don't Let it Happen Again" (1934), "Ev'ry Day Away from You" (1929), "My Confession" (1942), "Back in Your Own Backyard" (1928) "Singing a Vagabond Song" (1930) and perhaps the best of all his covers, "Underneath the Harlem Moon" (1932).

Other artists of the period include Wendy Baer, E. Morgan, Dunk, Gillam, and Hutof. Some of the artists resorted to using just their initials, but as the thirties began, more and more of the work just went unsigned. One of the main reasons was that the cover was no longer an inviting canvas for an artist but simply a paste-up board for the layout technician to put together a black-and-white photograph of a performer and work in a few graphics around it. And, just as importantly, Hollywood was taking over, and the covers were now being used as posters for the film. After the producer had put in the film's logo, mentioned its stars, its director, writers and wardrobe mistresses, there wasn't much room left for the artist.

Ukulele chords were a feature for music of the twenties. 1927.

A Leff cover for a Hollywood promotion that combines art deco with a touch of cubism. 1930.

But sheet music cover art belongs in the gallery of American folk art. Its time has past, but when more years have covered it over, we may well see collections of Starmer, or Barbelle, or Leff hanging proudly from the walls of our folk art museums.

Although the art form seems to have sputtered out in the late thirties when the cover styles, and needs, changed, the cover art began on a high note. Marian Klamkin in her book, *Old Sheet Music*, points out a little known fact that the great American painter Winslow Homer worked for the lithographer Bufford between 1855 and 1857 and illustrated sheet music covers during that time. "An early Homer design," she writes "signed with the initials, is the illustration on the cover of, the Wheelbarrow Polka.' The cover shows Major Benjamin Perly Poore pushing a wheelbarrow of apples from Newbury to Boston after having lost an election bet with Colonel Robert I. Burbank. When Poore reached his destination . . . there were thirty thousand onlookers to greet him."

Klamkin also notes that Nathaniel Currier, half of the team of Currier and Ives, was also a sheet music cover artist at one point in his long and distinguished career. From 1835 to 1839, when he was in business for himself, he turned a dollar or two by designing sheet music. The covers are signed and collectors who have them hang on to them for dear life.

America's favorite illustrator, Norman Rockwell, is also to be seen on sheet music covers. He did the famous cover for George M. Cohan's "Over There" and also did the art for "Little Grey Mother of Mine," "Down Where the Lillies Grow," and, later on in his career, "Lady Bird Cha Cha Cha."

There are some oddities, too. James Montgomery Flagg and Albert Vargas have been known to do covers. Flagg was the famous recruitment poster artist of World War I, as well as an illustrator of sweet young things in the early twenties. World War II G.I.'s will recall Vargas' pinup girls.

The combination of the music itself—which reflects the musical tastes of the time—coupled with the cover art—which reflects the artistic taste of the time—is another reason why sheet music collectors feel that they have a pretty good approach to the preservation, and understanding, of Americana through the years.

Starmer worked in design, an illustration and a performer for this standard. 1919.

Says Klamkin, "Music covers have been our earliest and most consistent form of decorative packaging."

CHAPTER X

A Word on the Price List

The following section on prices for sheet music is designed only to indicate a level of prices that I have encountered in buying, selling, and collecting music. Like any other antique, or collectible, a price for an item often is what you can get for it. If a collector can come across someone who will sell him the large, handsomely decorated colored sheet music from the turn of the century for twenty-five cents apiece, fine; that's the price, and buy all you can get. That will happen occasionally and it's the lure that keeps collectors and dealers forever searching.

Price lists and literature, for that matter, are uneven and hard to find, and not always reliable. The music is beginning to catch on, though, and soon it will be a staple among antique dealers. There will be other books following this one. Like the dealer's favorite refrain, "They're not making them any more," in the case of sheet music, that's almost true. Suffice it to say that if the music is in good condition, is pre-World War II, and it's selling for under two dollars, you can't go too wrong in buying it. Next year, it will be worth more, and the year after, still more.

Serious collection is still in its infancy, but there are some organizations that exchange auction and want lists and provide forums for collectors to talk and deal with each other. H. W. Cole Enterprise (P.O. Box 19004, Portland, Oregon 97219) issues auction lists and a useful publication on collecting called the "Enterprise Report." Some of the prices in this list come from Cole's auction experience. Mrs. Grace Friar (12 Grafton Street, Greenlaw, New York 11740)

ALL'S FAIR IN LOVE AND WAR

Music and Lyrics by
Harry Warren & Al
Dubin and Harold
Arlen & E.Y. Harburg

Warner Bros. Pictures, Inc.
present

DICK
POWELL

JOAN
BLONDELL

GOLD DIGGERS OF 1937

with
VICTOR MOORE
GLENDA FARRELL · LEE
DIXON · OSGOOD
PERKINS · ROSALIND
MARQUIS · Directed
by LLOYD BACON

HARMS
NEW YORK

Dick Powell fans collect Hollywood sheet music such as tunes from *Gold Diggers of 1937*. 1936.

publishes want lists, too. The National Sheet Music Society (P.O. Box 2235, Pasadena, California 91105) publishes a newsletter and directory that allows members to exchange price lists and want lists. Like most collectors, these enthusiasts are anxious to work with other collectors and welcome inquiries.

The prices indicated for each tune on the following list are not theoretical prices but ones that are actually from the marketplace. They are prices of music traded in shops, mostly in the Middle Atlantic and New England areas and were the prices most prevalent when this book was written (the latter part of 1976).

Other sources of pricing are the lists

of mail order collectors and dealers who are constantly exchanging music and thus represent a kind of musical stock exchange where price levels rise and fall—how seldom they fall!—according to demand and scarcity.

There is a general pattern to the prices that dealers quote. The antiquity is the prime factor, as it is in most collectibles. Obviously a tune from 1846, however undistinguished its rhyme or meter, or how forgettable its composer, is going to be worth more than a piece of music from 1940. The 1846 tune did not get a wide circulation and if several thousand were printed that was a lot. But the 1940 entry, if it was a moderately successful tune, was run off in the hundreds of thousands.

There are added increments of value for the factors discussed earlier: the cover artist, the name value of the performer on the cover, Jolson, Vallee, or Temple, for instance; and the endless splinter groups who collect songs about trains or autos, or the South, or what have you.

Since there are some hundreds of thousands of pieces of sheet music in circulation, no one index can be complete. But collectors and dealers can get an approximate idea of the worth of a piece of music if it's in the same group relative to year, size, artist, etc., as a piece of music that is identified and priced in this list.

The price list in this book, for instance, shows "There's a Small Hotel" by Rodgers and Hart. It's priced at $1. It was from the 1936 Broadway show, *On Your Toes,* and starred Ray Bolger. Another tune from the show was the title song, "On Your Toes," and, like "Small Hotel," it shows Bolger on the cover and lists the usual credits for the

The list of songs from a musical was often listed on the cover of sheet music. 1940.

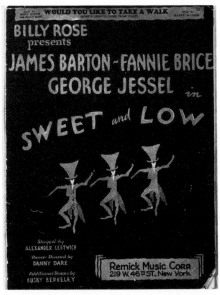

The Broadway theater has always been a major source of supply for sheet music publishers. 1930.

show. All of the songs from the show, in fact, have the same cover, with the only change being the top line that describes the tune and, of course, the appropriate music inside. Thus, if a collector doesn't have "Small Hotel" but has "On Your Toes" he can consider it to be in the same price category, or $1.

The assumption with the items in this price list is that they are all in good condition. That is, they have all their pages, there are no defacing tears, and are usable and legible in every respect. A small tear here or there, or the name of the original purchaser written across the music, doesn't really hurt. After all, it's an antique, and some wear and tear is merely the patina of authenticity.

CHAPTER XI

THE PRICE LIST

ABA DABA HONEYMOON. Fields & Donovan. 1914. $4

ACCENT ON YOUTH. Seymour & Lawnhurst. 1935. $2

AC-CENT-TCHU-ATE THE POSITIVE. Mercer & Arlen. 1944. $2

ACROSS THE ALLEY FROM THE ALAMO. Greene. 1947. $1

ACROSS THE CONTINENT. Jean Schwartz. 1900. $6

ACROSS THE RIO GRANDE. Redd, Graff & Ball. 1914. $3

ADORABLE. Marion & Whiting. 1933. $3

ADORATION. Richard 1. Weaver. 1911. $3

AFTER MY LAUGHTER CAME TEARS. Tobias & Turk. 1928. $1

AFTER SUNDOWN. Freed & Brown. 1933. $2

AFTER THE WAR IS OVER WILL THERE BE ANY HOME SWEET HOME. Pourmon & Woodruff.
  1919. $2

AH, BUT IS IT LOVE? Harberg & Gerney. 1933. $2

AH, SO PURE. Flotow. 1938. $2

AIN'T WE GOT FUN? Whiting, Egan & Kahn. 1921. $3

AIN'T YOU COMING BACK TO DIXIELAND. Egan & Whiting. 1918. $3

ALABAMA LULLABY. Cal DeVall. 1919. $2

(THE) ALCOHOLIC BLUES. Laska & Von Tilzer. 1919. $2

ALEXANDER DON'T YOU LOVE YOUR BABY NO MORE? Sterling & Von Tilzer. 1904. $4

ALL ALONE AND LONELY. Schwartz, Pearson, & Sanders. 1941. $1

ALL ASHORE. Billy Hill. 1931. $2

ALL BY MYSELF. Irving Berlin. 1921. $2

ALL BY YOURSELF IN THE MOONLIGHT. Jay Wallis. 1928. $1

ALL I DO IS DREAM OF YOU. Freed & Brown. 1934. $3

ALL OVER NOTHING AT ALL. Brennan, Cunningham & Rule. 1922. $3

ALL SHE'D SAY WAS UMH-HUM. Emery, Zany & Schenck. 1920. $3

ALL THE QUAKERS ARE SHOULDER SHAKERS. Kalmar, Leslie & Wendling. $3

ALL'S FAIR IN LOVE AND WAR. Warren, Dubin, Arlen & Harburg. 1936. $2

ALONE. Jones, Freed & Brown. 1935. $2

(THE) ALPHABET OF LOVE BEGINS AND ENDS WITH YOU. Gottleib, Mercer & Gensler. 1932. $2

ALTHOUGH I'M DOWN IN TENNESSEE, MY HEART IS UP IN MAINE. Fields & Scannell. 1914. $2

ALWAYS. Irving Berlin. 1925. $2

ALWAYS IN ALL WAYS. Robin, Whiting & Harling. 1930. $2

ALWAYS THE SAME SWEET PAL. Weinberg & Stone. 1928. $2

AM I A PASSING FANCY. Silver, Sherman & Lewis. 1929. $2

AM I BLUE? Clarke & Akst. 1929. $2

AM I THE ONE? Vallee & West. 1930. $2

AMERICA, HERE'S MY BOY. Sterling & Lange. 1917. $3

AMERICA I LOVE YOU. Leslie & Gettler. 1915. $3

AMERICA, OUR PRIDE. Louis Oesterle. 1917. $3

AMERICAN CITIZEN WALTZ. Frank Witmark. 1898. $7

AND MIMI. Kennedy & Simon. 1947. $1

AND SO TO BED. Mercer & Dolan. 1946. $1

AND THEN. Bryan & Paley. 1913. $3

ANGELS OF THE NIGHT. Harry Lincoln. 1909. $6

ANNABELLE. Brown & Henderson. 1923. $2

ANNIVERSARY. Dubin & Franklin. 1941. $1

ANNIVERSARY SONG. Jolson & Chaplin. 1946. $1

ANY OLD PLACE THE GANG GOES I'LL BE THERE. Wm. McKennan. 1918. $2

ANYTHING IS NICE IF IT COMES FROM DIXIELAND. Clarke, Meyer & Ager. 1919. $3

ANYTHING TO MAKE YOU HAPPY. Buddy Valentine. 1927. $2

(AN) APPLE BLOSSOM WEDDING. Kennedy & Simon. 1947. $1

APPLE SAUCE. Lyman, Arnheim & Freed. 1922. $1

APRIL IN PORTUGAL. Kennedy & Ferrdo. 1947. $1

APRIL PLAYED THE FIDDLE. Burke & Monaco. 1940. $2

ARE YOU ASHAMED OF ME? Lerner & Hoffman. 1930. $1

ARE YOU FROM HEAVEN? Gilbert & Friedland. 1917. $2

ARE YOU HAPPY? Yellen & Ager. 1927. $1

ARE YOU LONESOME TO-NIGHT? Turk & Handman. 1927. $1

ARE YOU READY TO FIGHT FOR YOUR COUNTRY? Woodburn & Miller. 1917. $3

ARE YOU SINCERE? Bryan & Gumble. 1908. $4

ARMY AND NAVY. Edmund Braham. 1911. $3

(THE) ARMY OF HALF-STARVED MEN. Paul Dresser. 1902. $12

ARRAH GO ON I'M GONNA GO BACK TO OREGON. Young, Lewis & Grant. 1916. $3

AS THE LUSITANIA WENT DOWN. Lamb & Klickman. 1915. $3

AS TIME GOES BY. Herman Hupfeld. 1931. $2

AS YOU DESIRE ME. Allie Wrubel. 1932. $2

AT DAWNING. Chas. Wakefield Cadmen. 1906. $4

ATLANTA. Skylar & Shaftol. 1945. $1

AT LAST. Gordon & Warren. 1942. $1

AT THE END OF THE ROAD. MacDonald & Hanley. 1924. $2

AT THE RAGTIME BALL. Lewis & Monaco. 1911. $3

AU REVOIR BUT NOT GOOD BYE (SOLDIER BOY). Brown & Von Tilzer. 1917. $3

AVALON. Jolson & Rose. 1920. $6

AVALON TOWN. Clake & Brown. 1928. $1

AWAY DOWN SOUTH IN HEAVEN. Green & Warren. 1927. $1

BABY. Kahn & Van Alstyne. 1919. $2

BABY FEET GO PITTER PATTER. Gus Kahn. 1927. $2

BABY GIRL KAREN ANN. Harold Mahon. 1953. $1

BABY-OH WHERE CAN YOU BE? Koehler & Magine. 1929. $1

BABY ROSE. Weslyn & Christie. 1911. $3

BACK, BACK, BACK TO BALTIMORE. Williams & Van Alstyne. 1904. $3

BACK IN YOUR OWN BACK YARD. Jolson, Rose & Dreyer. 1928. $2

BACK TO DIXIELAND. Jack Yellen. 1914. $2

BACK TO THE CAROLINA YOU LOVE. Clarke & Schwartz. 1914. $3

BALLIN' THE JACK. Chris Smith. 1914. $8

BAM BAM BAMY SHORE. Dixon & Henderson. 1925. $3

BATTLE CRY OF FREEDOM. John W. Schaum. 1944. $1

(THE) BATTLE SONG OF LIBERTY. Bigelow & Yellen. 1917. $2

BE MY LOVE. Cahn & Brodazky. 1950. $1

BE STILL MY HEART. Glynn & Egan. 1934. $1

BEALE STREET MAMA. Turk & Robinson. 1923. $2

BEAUTIFUL. Gillespie & Shay. 1927. $2

BEAUTIFUL. Leonard & Stein. 1929. $2

BEAUTIFUL DIXIE ROSE. McKeon & Gutman. 1912. $4

BEAUTIFUL DREAMER. Stephen C. Foster. 1864. $17

BEAUTIFUL EGGS. Bryan & Paley. 1914. $3

BEAUTIFUL EYES. Whiting, DeHaven & Snyder. 1909. $5

(A) BEAUTIFUL LADY IN BLUE. Lewis & Coots. 1935. $1

BEAUTIFUL OHIO. Earl & MacDonald. 1918. $3

BEAUTY MUST BE LOVED. Fain & Kahal. 1934. $2

BECAUSE DEAR HEART, 'TIS YOU I LOVE. Marie White. 1911. $3

BECAUSE THEY ALL LOVE YOU. Malie & Little. 1924. $1

BEGIN THE BEGUINE. Cole Porter. 1944. $2

BEG YOUR PARDON. Craig & Smith. 1947. $2

BEI MIR BIST DU SHOEN. Jacobs, Secunda, Cahn & Chaplin. 1937. $2

BELIEVE IT OR NOT (IT'S ALWAYS YOU). McCarthy & Monaco. 1929. $2

(THE) BELLE OF NEW YORK. Morton & Kerke. 1929. $2

BENEATH THE PINES OF MAINE. Walter Rolfe. 1901. $6

BESIDE AN OPEN FIREPLACE. Denniker & Osborne. 1929. $1

BESIDE THE SUNSET TRAIL. Whiting, Goodhart & Hoffman. 1932. $3

BESIDE YOU. Livingston & Evans. 1946. $1

BETTY CO-ED. Fogarty & Vallee. 1930. $1

BETWEEN A KISS AND A SIGH. Burke & Johnston. 1938. $2

BEYOND THE BLUE HORIZON. Robin & Whiting. 1930. $1

BIDIN' MY TIME. George and Ira Gershwin. 1930. $2

BILL. Hammerstein & Kern Harms. 1927. $2

BILLY. Goodwin, Kendis & Paley. 1911. $2

BING! BANG! BING'EM ON THE RHINE. Mahoney & Flynn. 1918. $2

(THE) BLARNEY STONE. Hennaway & Lauder. 1913. $2

BLESS YOU. Lane & Baker. 1939. $1.

BLOSSOM TIME. Willner & Reichert. 1921. $3

BLUE. Clarke, Leslie & Handman. 1922. $1

(THE) BLUE AND THE GRAY. Paul Dresser. 1900. $6

BLUE BELL. Madden & Morse. 1904. $4

BLUE DIAMONDS. Caddigan & Story. 1920. $3

BLUE FEATHER. Theodore Morse. 1909. $5

BLUE GRASS. DeSylva, Brown & Henderson. 1928. $3

BLUE JEANS. Kerr & Traveller. 1920. $1

BLUE RIVER. Bryan & Meyer. 1927. $2

BLUE SKIRT WALTZ. Parish & Blaha. 1944. $2

BLUEBIRDS IN THE MOONLIGHT. Robin & Rainger. 1939. $1

BLUE-EYED BLUES. Billy Fazioli. 1922. $3

BLUES IN THE NIGHT. Mercer & Arlen. 1941. $2

BLUES MY NAUGHTY SWEETIE GIVES TO ME. Swanstone, McCarren & Morgan. 1919. $2

THE BOGEY MAN IS HERE. Leonard & Stern. 1929. $1.

BOO-HOO. Hayman, Carmen, Lombardo & Loeb. 1937. $2

BOSTON TOWN. Marsh & Rice. 1907. $3

(THE) BOWERY. Hoyt & Gaunt. 1935. $1

BOY O'MINE GOOD NIGHT. Burr & Wilson. 1918. $2

(THE) BOYS ARE COMING HOME. Edwin Taylot. 1919. $2

(THE) BRAVEST HEART OF ALL. Egan & Whiting. 1917. $2

BRIGHT EYES. Smith, Motzan & Jerome. 1920. $3

BRIGHT EYES. Dickson, Hauerbach & Hoschna. 1919. $3

(THE) BROADWAY. T. F. Morse. 1895. $3

BROADWAY CABALLERO. Russell & Stewart. 1941. $1

BROADWAY MELODY. Freed & Brown. 1929. $2

BROADWAY ROSE. West, Fried & Spencer. 1920. $1

(THE) BROOKLYN LIGHT GUARD QUICKSTEP. Alla Dodworth. 1839. $22

BROWN EYES WHY ARE YOU BLUE? Meyer & Bryan. 1925. $2

BUILD A LITTLE HOME. Dubin & Warren. 1933. $2

BUT I DO—YOU KNOW I DO. Kahn & Donaldson. 1926. $1

BUT WHERE ARE YOU? Irving Berlin. 1936. $2

BUTTONS AND BOWS. Livingston & Evans. 1943. $1

BUY A BOND BUY A BOND FOR LIBERTY. 1918. $3

BUY A KISS. Burton, Jason & Steiner. 1933. $2

BY A WATERFALL. Kahal & Fain. 1933. $2

BY THE CAMPFIRE. Girling & Wenrigh. 1919. $2

BY THE RIVER OF ROSES. Symes & Burke. 1943. $1

BY THE SAPPHIRE SEA. Ted Snyder. 1922. $3

BYE AND BYE SWEETHEART. Yellen, Valentine & Ford. 1928. $3

BYE BYE BLACKBIRD. Dixon & Henderson. 1926. $3

BYE-BYE PRETTY BABY. Gardner & Hamilton. 1927. $1

CABIN IN THE SKY. Latouche & Duke. 1940. $1

(THE) CAISSONS GO ROLLING ALONG. E. L. Gruber. 1931. $2

CALIFORNIA. Friend & Conrad. 1922. $3

CALIFORNIA AND YOU. Leslie & Puck. 1914. $3

CALL IT ANYTHING (IT WASN'T LOVE). Fred Fisher. 1934. $2

CALL ME BACK, PAL O' MINE. Perricone & Dixon. 1921. $2

CALL ME UP SOME RAINY AFTERNOON. Irving Berlin. 1918. $9

CAMPIN' ON DE OLE SUWANEE. L. O. Smith. 1899. $35

CAN I FORGET YOU? Kern & Hammerstein. 1937. $1

CAN YOU KEEP A SECRET? Maurice Dunlap. 1916. $4

CANARY ISLE. Ben Schwartz. 1922. $3

CAN'T HELP LOVING DAT MAN OF MINE. Hammerstein & Kern. 1927. $2

CAROLINE, I'M COMING BACK TO YOU. Caddigan & McHugh. 1916. $3

CAROLINA MAMMY. Billy James. 1922. $1

CAROLINA MINE. Friend & Rosoff. 1926. $2

CAROLINA MOON. Davis & Burke. 1928. $2

CAROLINA SUNSHINE. Hirsch & Schmidt. 1919. $3

CAROLINA SWEETHEART. Billy James. 1925. $2

'CAUSE I'M IN LOVE. Walter Donaldson. 1928. $1

'CAUSE MY BABY SAYS IT'S SO. Warren & Dubin. 1937. $2

CHANT OF THE JUNGLE. Freed & Brown. 1929. $2

CHANTICLEER (COOK-A-DOODLE-OO) RAG. M. Gumble. 1910

CHAPEL OF THE ROSES. Harris & Baer. 1951. $1

CHARITY BEGINS AT HOME. Moss & Denslow. 1915. $3

CHARMING. Grey & Stothart. 1929. $3

CHASING SHADOWS. Davis & Silver. 1935. $2

CHEER UP FATHER, CHEER UP MOTHER. Bryan & Paley. 1910. $3

CHEERFUL LITTLE EARFUL. Gershwin, Rose & Warren. 1930. $2

CHICKERY CHICK. Dee & Lippman. 1945. $1

CHIMES OF VENICE. R. G. Gradi. 1912. $4

CHINESE LULLABY. Robert H. Bowers. 1919. $3

CHINESE MOON. Bronfin & Nussbaum. 1926. $1

CHLO-E. Kahn & Moret. 1927. $2

CIRCUS DAY IN DIXIE. Yellen & Gumble. 1915. $3

CITY CALLED HEAVEN. Bob Warner. 1941. $1

CLAPA YO HANDS. George and Ira Gershwin. 1930. $3

CLOSE TO YOUR HEART. Billy Heagney. 1927. $2

CLOUDS. Kahn & Donaldson. 1935. $1

(A) COACH AND FOUR. Livingston & Evans. 1946. $2

COCKTAILS FOR TWO. Johnston & Coslow. 1934. $2

COFFEE IN THE MORNING AND KISSES IN THE NIGHT. Dubin & Warren. 1933. $2

COLUMBIA THE GEM OF THE OCEAN. David T. Shaw. 1843. $25

COME BACK TO ME. David, Frogson & Christine. 1910. $3

COME ON OVER HERE IT'S A WONDERFUL PLACE. Jerome & Furth. 1916. $3

COME TAKE A TRIP IN MY AIR SHIP. Evans & Shields. 1904. $7

COME TO ME LOVE AT TWILIGHT. Effie Henderson. 1914. $3

COMIN' IN ON A WING AND A PRAYER. Adamson & McHugh. 1943. $2

(THE) CONTINENTAL. Magidson & Conrad. 1934. $1

COOL WATER. Bob Nolan. 1936. $1

CORN FLOWER. Chas. Coote. 1842. $26

COTTON PICKIN' TIME IN DIXIELAND. McCane & Haward. 1913. $4

COULD BE. Mercer & Donaldson. 1938. $1

COULD THE DREAMS OF A DREAMER COME TRUE? Branson & Lange. 1915. $2

COUNT THE DAYS. Tilson & Bason. 1922. $2

COUNTING THE DAYS. Zaret & Kramer. 1945. $1

CREOLE BELLES. J. Bodewalt Lampe. 1900. $5

CRICKET POLKA. Wm. Withers. 1863. $16

Before World War I

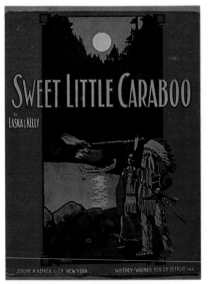

Typical Indian intermezzo with a Starmer cover. 1904.

Berlin and railroads were big back then. 1912.

The humorous art and performer's photograph were typical. 1902.

Europe was O.K. but there was no place like the U.S.A. 1909.

Nineteenth Century Sheet Music Covers

1850.

1850.

1859.

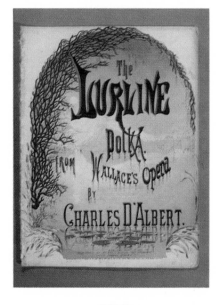

1860.

Used Color and Art to Sell the Music

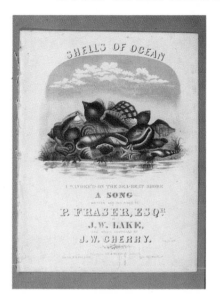

1860.

1864.

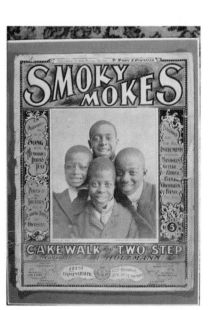

1899.

1899.

The Twenties And Thirties

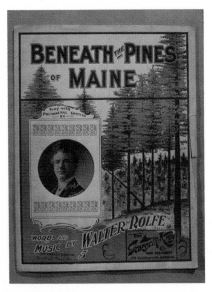

Songs about states were big sellers. 1927.

Typical Hollywood cover promotion. 1936.

Pretty girls sold sheet music, too. 1925

Hudiacoff was the artist. 1924.

CROSS YOUR HEART. Gensler & DeSylva. 1926. $2

CRUISING DOWN THE RIVER. Beadell & Tollerton. 1945. $1

CRYING FOR THE CAROLINES. Lewis, Young & Warren. 1930. $2

CRYING MYSELF TO SLEEP. Klenner & Wendling. 1930. $2

(THE) CURSE OF AN ACHING HEART. Fink & Piantadosi. 1913. $2

DADDY LONG LEGS. Gleeson & Von Tilzer. 1919. $2

DADDY MINE. Wilson & Dubin. 1918. $3

DADDY'S WONDERFUL PAL. Freedman, Nelson & Link. 1923. $2

DAISIES WON'T TELL. Anita Owen. 1908. $7

DANCING WITH MY SHADOW. Harry Woods. 1934. $2

DANCING WITH TEARS IN MY EYES. Dubin & Burke. 1930. $2

DAPPER DAN. Von Tilzer & Brown. 1921. $6

DARDANELLA. Bernard, Black & Fisher. 1919. $2

(THE) DAUGHTER OF ROSIE O'GRADY. Brice & Donaldson. 1918. $2

DEAR EYES THAT HAUNT ME. Smith & Kalman. 1927. $2

DEAR OLD DADDY LONG LEGS. Fleeson & Von Tilzer. 1919. $3

DEAR OLD GIRL. Buck & Morse. 1903. $6

DEAR OLD PAL OF MINE. Robe & Rice. 1918. $3

DE CAMPTOWN RACES. Stephen Foster. 1940. $1

DEEP IN MY HEART, DEAR. Donnelly & Romberg. 1925. $2

DEEP PURPLE. Parish & De Rose. 1934. $2

DENVER TOWN. Breen & Botsford. 1908. $3

(THE) DESERT SONG. Harbach & Hammerstein. 1926. $3

DIANE. Rapee & Pollack. 1927. $1

DID I REMEMBER? Adamson & Donaldson. 1936. $1

DID YOU EVER SEE A DREAM WALKING. Gordon & Revel. 1933. $2

DID YOU MEAN IT? Baker, Silvers & Lyman. 1927. $2

DIME A DOZEN. Cindy Walker. 1949. $1

DINNER FOR ONE, PLEASE JAMES. Michael Carr. 1935. $1

DIXIE DOODLE. Zirkel & McCullough. 1916. $3

DIXIE'S LAND. Charles Brobe. 1860. $17

DO YOU EVER THINK OF ME. Kerr, Cooper & Burtnett. 1920. $2

DOES IT PAY? Zittel & Sutton. 1907. $6

DOES YOUR HEART BEAT FOR ME? Parish, Morgan & Johnson. 1936. $1

DOLL DANCE. Nacio Herb Brown. 1926. $1

DOLL HOUSE. Wynn, Richman & Davis. 1921. $2

DOLLY MCHUGH. Wardell & Pollack. 1914. $5

DOLORES. Loesser & Alter. 1941. $1

(THE) DONKEY SERENADE. Friml, Stothart, Wright & Forrest. 1937. $2

DON'T BE A CRY BABY. Robin & Rainger. 1933. $2

DON'T BE ANGRY. Lewis & Weeks. 1934. $2

DON'T BELIEVE EVERYTHING YOU DREAM. Adamson & McHugh. 1943. $2

DON'T BE LIKE THAT. Gottler, Tobias & Pinkard. 1928. $2

DON'T BE SORROWFUL, DARLING. Cary & Webster. 1862. $12

DON'T BITE THE HAND THAT'S FEEDING YOU. Heier & Morgan. 1915. $4

DON'T BLAME ME. Fields & McHugh. 1933. $3

DON'T CRY JOE. Joe Marsala. 1949. $1

DON'T FENCE ME IN. Cole Porter. 1944. $1

DON'T GIVE UP THE SHIP. Warren & Dubin. 1935. $2

DON'T HOLD EVERYTHING. DeSylva, Brown & Henderson. 1928. $2

DON'T LET IT HAPPEN AGAIN. Symes, Neiburg & Levinson. 1934. $2

DON'T SWEETHEART ME. Friend & Tobias. 1943. $1

DON'T TAKE ADVANTAGE. Rogers & Monaco. 1919. $3

DON'T TAKE MY DARLING BOY AWAY. Dillon & Von Tilzer. 1915. $2

DON'T PUT A TAX ON THE BEAUTIFUL GIRLS. Yellen & Agers. 1918. $2

DON'T SAVE YOUR LOVE FOR A RAINY DAY. Buollock & Spina. 1937. $1

DON'T SAY GOODBY IF YOU LOVE ME. Davis & Dodd. 1936. $1

DON'T WORRY. Gannon & Styne. 1943. $1

DOT BEAUTIFUL HEBREW GIRL. Neeler & Schleifarth. 1881. $15

DOUBLE CLOG DANCE. J.L.G. 1864. $45

DOWN BY THE RIVER. Creamer & Layton. 1923. $3

DOWN IN BOM - BOMBAY. MacDonald & Carroll. 1915. $3

DOWN IN THE SUBWAY. Schwartz & Jerome. 1904. $4

DOWN OLD INDIANA WAY. Wagner & De Costa. 1911. $4

DOWN THE RIVER OF GOLDEN DREAMS. Klenner & Shilkret. 1930. $1

DOWN WHERE THE SWANEE RIVER FLOWS. Caron, Alberte & Von Tilzer. 1916. $3

DOWN YONDER. L. Wolfe Gilbert. 1921. $3

DREAM DADDY. Herscher & Keefer. 1923. $1

DREAM, DREAM, DREAM. Redmon & Ricca. 1946. $1

DREAM LOVER. Schertzinger & Grey. 1929. $2

DREAMY MELODY. Koehler, Magino & Naset. 1922. $2

DREAM MOTHER. Lewis, Sherman & Burke. 1929. $1

(A) DREAM OF LOVE. Woods & Madden. 1907. $6

DREAM TRAIN. Newan & Baskette. 1928. $3

DREAMY ALABAMA. MacDonald & Earl. 1919. $2

DRIFTING ALONG TO THE ISLE OF LOVE. Weeks & Alexander. 1920. $6

DRIFTWOOD. Kahn & Gold. 1924. $1

DRIFTWOOD. Davis, Davis & Lyman. 1928. $1

DRINKING SONG. Donnelly & Romberg. 1925. $2

DUNGAREE DOLL! Raleigh & Edwards. 1940. $1

(THE) DYING POET. L.M. Gottschalk. 1907. $5

EACH BOY IS A HERO. E.B. Myers. 1918. $3

EACH LITTLE FEELING. Dempsey & Schmidt. 1912. $2

EACH STITCH IS A THOUGHT OF YOU, DEAR. Sweet & Baskette. 1918. $2

EBB TIDE. Robin & Rainger. 1937. $1

(THE) ECHOES OF MY ROCKY MOUNTAIN HOME. 1904. $5

EENY MEENY MINEY MO. Mercer & Malneck. 1935. $2

EGOSTISTICAL EVA. Blanche Merrill. 1910. $3

ELAINE MY MOVING PICTURE QUEEN. Elbert & Wesley. 1915. $4

ELIZA. Kahn & Fiorito. 1924. $1

EMPTY SADDLES. Billy Hill, Shapiro & Bernstein. 1936. $1

EVELINA. Arlen & Harburg. 1944. $2

EVERY LITTLE BIT ADDED TO WHAT YOU'VE GOT. Dillion Bros. 1907. $5

EVERYBODY TAP. Yellen & Ager. 1929. $2

EVERYBODY WANTS A KEY TO MY CELLAR. Rose, Baskett & Pollack. 1919. $5

EVERYBODY'S BUDDY. Grossman & Frisch. 1920. $3

EVERYTIME. Frank Beaston. 1923. $2

EV'RY DAY AWAY FROM YOU. Tobias & Miller. 1929. $2

EV'RYONE SAYS I LOVE YOU. Kalmar & Ruby. 1932. $2

EV'RYTHING I LOVE. Cole Porter. 1941. $2

(I'VE GOT) EV'RYTHING THAT GOES WITH LOVE. Lavan, Mitchell, James & Seitter. 1933. $3

(A) FADED SUMMER LOVE. Phil Baxter. 1931. $3

FAIRY WEDDING WALTZ. J. Turner. 1907. $5

FAITHFUL FOREVER. Robin & Rainger. 1939. $1

FALLING. Collins, Cameron & Fields. 1922. $2

FALLING STAR. Bayes & Norworth. 1918. $3

FAR AWAY IN SUNNY GEORGIA. Alexander Mitchell. 1906. $5

FAR AWAY PLACES. Whitney & Kramer. 1948. $1

(THE) FARMER TOOK ANOTHER LOAD AWAY HAY! HAY! Leslie, O'Flynn & Vincent. 1925. $6

FASCINATING RHYTHM. George & Ira Gershwin. 1924. $3

FASCINATION. Louis Silvers. 1922. $2

FATE. Byron Gay. 1922. $2

FEATHER HEAD. Gallop, Kuhn & Shaw. 1944. $1

FEATHER YOUR NEST. Kendis, Brockman & Johnson. 1920. $3

(THE) FINE OLD ENGLISH GENTLEMAN. Atwill's Saloon. 1850. $25

(THE) FINEST FLAG THAT FLIES. Hughes & Richardson. 1914. $1

FIRE DRILL. Harry Lincoln. 1919. $5

(THE) FIRST GUN IS FIRED. 1861. $40

(THE) FIRST LOVE LETTER POLKA. Chas. Foydel. 1860. $27

(THE) FIRST TIME I SAW YOU. Wrubel & Shilkret. 1937. $2

FIT AS A FIDDLE. Freed, Hoffman & Goodheart. 1932. $2

FIVE MINUTES MORE. Cahn & Styne. 1946. $1

FLAG THAT TRAIN. Richmond, Rothschild & McPhail. 1925. $5

FLOATING DOWN THE RIVER. Lewis & White. 1913. $6

FLORENCE SWEET. J. H. McNaughton. 1867. $22

FLOW ALONG RIVER TENNESSEE. Bryan, Gumble & Wells. 1913. $3

FLYING ARROW. Abe Holzman. 1906. $3

FOLLOW THE SWALLOW. Rose, Dixon & Henderson. 1924. $3

FOLLOWING THE SUN AROUND. McCarthy & Tierney. 1926. $3

(A) FOOL IN LOVE. McQueen & Lippman. 1933. $3

FOR ALL WE KNOW. Lewis & Coots. 1934. $2

FOR DIXIE AND UNCLE SAM. Brennan & Ball. 1916. $3

FOREVER AND FOREVER. Rosa & Winkler. 1947. $1

FORGETTING YOU. DeSylva, Brown & Henderson. 1928. $1

FORGIVE ME. Yellen & Ager. 1927. $1

FOR KILLARNEY AND YOU. Walsh & Teasdale. 1910. $4

FOR ME AND MY GAL. Leslie, Goetz & Meyer. 1917. $3

FOR SENTIMENTAL REASONS. Watson & Best. 1946. $1

FOR THE FREEDOM OF THE WORLD. Cooke & Zamecnik. 1917. $3

FOUR WALLS. Jolson, Rose & Dreyer. 1927. $1

FRAT. John Barth. 1910. $4

FRECKLE FACE YOU'RE BEAUTIFUL. Friend & Lombardo. 1934. $2

FRECKLES. Hess, Johnson & Ager. 1919. $1

FRENESI. Charles & Russell. 1939. $1

FRESH AS A DAISY. Scholl & Rich. 1933. $2

(A) FRIEND OF YOURS. Burke & Van Heusen. 1944. $1

FULL MOON AND EMPTY ARMS. Kaye & Messman. 1946. $1

FUNNY. Yoell & Anderson. 1925. $1

FUZZY WUZZY. Hoffman, Drake & Livingston. 1944. $1

(A) GAL IN CALICO. Schwartz & Robin. 1946. $1

GALWAY BAY. T. Colahan. 1947. $1

(THE) GAMBLING MAN. Jerome & Schwartz. 1902. $15

(THE) GATES OF GLADNESS. Brennan, Cunningham & Rule. 1925. $3

GEE! AIN'T IT GREAT TO BE HOME. Phil Capwell. 1909. $4

GENERAL GRANT'S MARCH. E. Mack. 1862. $23

GENERAL MORGAN'S PARADE MARCH. C. L. Underner. 1859. $35

GEORGIA MOON. Berger & McCauley. 1915. $3

GERALDINE. Davis & Akst. 1927. $2

GERONIMO. Dempsey & Lilly. 1925. $3

GET OUT AND GET UNDER THE MOON. Tobias, Jerome & Shay. 1928. $2

(THE) GIRL OF THE GOLDEN WEST. Gillespie, Van Alstyne & Cooke. 1923. $2

(THE) GIRL WHO BROKE MY HEART. Dubin & Robinson. 1928. $1

GIVE YOURSELF A PAT ON THE BACK. Butler & Wallace. 1928. $3

GLAD RAG DOLL. Yellen, Ager & Dougherty. 1929. $3

GLORIANNA. Pollack & Clare. 1928. $2

GO HOME AND TELL YOUR MOTHER. Fields & McHugh. 1930. $2

GOD BE WITH OUR BOYS TONIGHT. Bowles & Sanderson. 1918. $3

GOD, SPARE OUR BOYS OVER THERE. Jerome & Mahoney. 1918. $3

GOING BACK H-O-M-E. Kenneth S. Clark. 1914. $3

GOING MY WAY. Burke & VanHeusen. 1944. $1

GOIN' TO THE COUNTY FAIR. Lessing & Cook. 1912. $3

GOLDEN ARROW. Williams & Van Alstyne. 1909. $5

GOLDEN DAYS. Donnell & Romberg. 1925. $2

GOLDEN GATE OPEN FOR ME. Kendis & Brockman. 1919. $2

GONE. Ley & David. 1922. $2

GOOD-BYE DOLLY GRAY. Cobb & Barnes. 1900. $7

GOOD BYE, GOOD LUCK, GOD BLESS YOU. Brennan & Ball. 1916. $3

GOOD BYE LITTLE GIRL GOOD BYE. Cobb & Edwards. 1904. $6

GOODBYE MY LADY LOVE. Jos. E. Howard. 1932. $2

GOODBYE SUNSHINE, HELLO MOON. Buck & Eckstein. 1919. $2

GOOD EVENIN'. Seymour, O'Flynn & Hoffman. 1930. $2

GOOD MORNING, DEARIE. Caldwell & Kern. 1921. $3

GOOD MORNING MR. ZIP, ZIP, ZIP. Robt. Floyd. 1918. $3

GOOD-NIGHT DEAR HEART. Eliz. M. Bacon. 1909. $5

GOOD NIGHT LITTLE GIRL OF MY DREAMS. Tobias & Burke. 1933. $1

GOOD NIGHT LOVELY LITTLE LADY. Gordon & Revel. 1934. $2

(THE) GOOD OLD USA. Drislane & Morse. 1906. $3

GOODY-GOODY. Mercer & Malneck. 1936. $1

GORGEOUS. Davis & Akst. 1927. $3

GOTTA BE THIS OR THAT. Sunny Skylar. 1945. $1

GOVERNOR MORGAN'S PAROLE MARCH. Wm. Cluett. 1859. $25

(THE) GREAT ROCK ISLAND ROUTE. J. A. Roff. 1882. $22

(A) HABIT OF MINE. Robin & Whiting. 1929. $3

HAIL TO THE REDSKINS. Griffith & Breeskin. 1938. $2

HAIR OF GOLD, EYES OF BLUE. S. Skylar. 1948. $1

HAND IN HAND. Lewis & Morgan. 1938. $1

(THE) HAND THAT ROCKS THE CRADLE RULES THE WORLD. Fleming & Holzman. 1905. $4

(A) HANDFUL OF STARS. Lawrence & Shapiro. 1940. $2

HANG YOUR HEART ON A HICKORY LIMB. Burke & Monaco. 1939. $2

HAPPY HANNAH. Theo. Havemeyer. 1898. $8

HAPPY IN LOVE. Yellen & Fain. 1941. $1

HARBOR LIGHTS. Kennedy & Williams. 1937. $1

HARVESTING. Everett & Jay. 1924. $3

HATS OFF HERE COMES A LADY. Young & Petkers. 1932. $2

HAVE I STAYED AWAY TOO LONG. F. Loesser. 1943. $1

HAVE YOU GOT ANY CASTLES, BABY? Whiting & Mercer. 1917. $4

HAVE YOU SEEN MY SWEETHEART IN HIS UNIFORM OF BLUE? Cobb & Edwards. 1902. $7

HAVIN' MYSELF A TIME. Robin & Rainger. 1938. $1

HAWAIIAN BUTTERFLY. Little, Naskette & Santly. 1917. $3

HE LAID AWAY A SUIT OF GRAY TO WEAR THE UNION BLUE. Wicke & Jansen. 1900. $6

HE WAS A SAILOR BOY BRAVE. Northey & Hanford. 1912. $3

HE WAS A SOLDIER FROM THE U. S. A. Lawton & Kocian. 1914. $4

HE WEARS A PAIR OF SILVER WINGS. Maschwitz & Carr. 1941. $1

HE WOOED HER. Harrington & Lopas. 1935. $2

HEAD OVER HEELS IN LOVE. Parsons & Thayer. 1926. $1

HEARTS AND FLOWERS. Theo. Tobain. 1921. $3

HEAVEN'S ARTILLERY. Harry Lincoln. 1904. $6

HEAV'N. Fanny G. Eckhardt. 1947. $1

HE'D HAVE TO GET UNDER — GET OUT AND GET UNDER. Clarke, Leslie & Abrahams. 1913. $4

HELLO CENTRAL GIVE ME HEAVEN. Chas. K. Harris 1937. $3

HELLO CENTRAL, GIVE ME NO MAN'S LAND. Lewis, Young & Schwartz. 1918. $3

HELLO HAWAII, HOW ARE YOU? Leslie, Kalmar & Schwartz. 1914 $3

HER LITTLE SOLDIER BOY. Madden & Jarden. 1906. $6

(THE) HERDSMAN'S MOUNTAIN SONG. "Pa Berget". Date unknown. $35

HERE COMES THE SANDMAN. Dubin & Warren. 1937. $3

HERE I AM. DeSylva, Brown & Henderson. 1926. $2

HERE IT IS MONDAY AND I'VE STILL GOT A DOLLAR LEFT. Sigler & Cleary. 1932. $2

HERE YOU ARE. Robin & Rainger. 1942. $1

HE'S HOME FOR A LITTLE WHILE. Goell & Shapiro. 1945. $1

HE'S NOT WORTH YOUR TEARS. Dixon, Rose & Warren. 1930. $2

HE'S THE LAST WORD. Kahn & Donaldson. 1927. $1

HI NELLIE. Dixon & Wrubel. 1934. $3

HIAWATHA. Moret & O'Dea. 1903. $4

HIAWATHA'S MELODY OF LOVE. Bryan, Mehlinger & Meyer. 1920. $2

HICKI HOY. Murphy & Muir. 1915. $4

HIGHLANDERS! FIX BAYONETS. Pitts & O'Hare. 1915. $5

HOLD ME. Hickman & Black. 1920. $2

HOLD ME CLOSE. Lee & Lillie. 1936. $1

HOLD YOUR MAN. Freed & Brown. 1933. $3

HOME AGAIN. Will J. White. 1917. $3

HOMEWARD BOUND. Johnson, Geetz & Meyer. 1917. $2

HONESTLY. Newman & Jones. 1933. $2

HONEY. Simons, Gillespie & Whiting. 1928. $2

HONEY-BABE. Webster & Steiner. 1954. $1

HONEY BABY WON'T YOU BE MINE? Johnson & Goetz. 1917. $3

HONEY BOY. Norworth & Von Tilzer. 1935. $1

HONEYMOON. Sherwood & Arden. 1919. $3

HONOLULU EYES. Johnson & Violinsky. 1920. $2

(AN) HOUR NEVER PASSES. Jimmy Kennedy. 1944. $1

HOW AM I TO KNOW. Parker & King. 1929. $2

HOW ARE THINGS IN GLOCCA MORRA. Harburg & Lane. 1946. $1

HOW CAN YOU SAY NO. Dubin, Kahal & Burke. 1932. $4

HOW DO YOU DO IT? Burke & Van Heusen. 1940. $1

HOW HIGH THE MOON. Hamilton & Lewis. 1940. $3

HOW LONG WILL IT LAST? Lief & Meyer. 1931. $4

HOW MANY TIMES? Irving Berlin. 1926. $2

HUCKLEBERRY FINN. Young, Hess & Lewis. 1917. $2

HUGGABLE, KISSABLE YOU. Irving Bibo. 1929. $3

HUMMING. Breau & Henderson. 1920. $2

HUMORESQUE. Coleman, Goetz, Bryan & Rosey. 1920. $3

(A) HUNDRED YEARS FROM NOW. Caddigan & Brennan. 1914. $5

HURT. Piantadosi & Solomon. 1930. $2

(THE) HUT-SUT SONG. Killion, McMichael & Owens. 1941. $1

I AM AN AMERICAN. Schuster, Cunningham & Whitcup. 1940. $1

I CALLED TO SAY GOODNIGHT. Young, Bachmann & Conrad. 1932. $3

I CAN WIGGLE MY EARS. Sigler, Goodhart & Hoffman. 1935. $2

I CANNOT BID HIM GANG, MITHER. McMaker & Knight. 1839. $40

I CAN'T BEGIN TO TELL YOU. Gordon & Monaco. 1945. $1

I CAN'T DO WITHOUT YOU. Irving Berlin. 1928. $2

I CAN'T ESCAPE FROM YOU. Robin & Whiting. 1936. $1

I CAN'T GET AWAY FROM YOU. Boone & Lang. 1931. $1

I CAN'T LOSE THAT LONGING FOR YOU. Dixon & Greer. 1936. $1

I CERTAINLY COULD. Yellen & Ager. 1926. $2

I COULD MAKE YOU CARE. Cahn & Chaplin. 1940. $3

I COULDN'T BELIEVE MY EYES. Sammels, Whitcup & Powell. 1935. $1

I COULDN'T SLEEP A WINK LAST NIGHT. Adamson & McHugh. 1943. $1

I COULDN'T TELL THEM WHAT TO DO. Turk & Lawnhurst. 1933. $2

I DIDN'T KNOW WHAT TIME IT WAS. Rodgers & Hart. 1939. $2

I DIDN'T RAISE MY BOY TO BE A SOLDIER. Bryan & Piantadosi. 1915. $3

I DON'T CARE WHO KNOWS IT. Adamson & McHugh. 1944. $1

I DON'T WANT TO GET WELL. Pease, Johnson & Tentes. 1917. $2

I DON'T WANT TO LOVE YOU. Henry Prichard. 1944. $1

I DREAM OF YOU. Goetschius & Osser. 1944. $1

I GUESS I'LL GET THE PAPERS AND GO HOME. Prince, Rogers & Kanner. 1946. $1

I GUESS I'LL SOON BE BACK IN DIXIELAND. Jack Rogers. 1915. $2

I HATE TO LOSE YOU I'M SO USED TO YOU NOW. Clarke & Gettler. 1918. $3

I HAVE EYES. Robin & Rainger. 1928. $3

I HAVE TO HAVE YOU. Robins & Whiting. 1929. $3

I HEAR A CALL TO ARMS. Coslow & Siegel. 1937. $1

I JUST CAME FROM DEAR OLD DIXIELAND. David Stamper. 1912. $2

I JUST KISSED YOUR PICTURE GOODNIGHT. Kent & David. 1942. $1

I LIKE IT THAT WAY. Conrad, Mitchell & Gottler. 1934. $2

I LOVE THE LAND OF OLD BLACK JOE. Clarke & Donaldson. 1921. $2

I LOVE TO WHISTLE. McHugh & Adamson. 1938. $2

I LOVE YOU. Cole Porter. 1943. $1

I LOVE YOU, BELIEVE ME I LOVE YOU. Cowan & Boutelye. 1929. $3

I LOVE YOU SO. Kahn & Fiorito. 1930. $3

I MAY BE DANCING WITH SOMEBODY ELSE. Little, Oppenheim & Shuster. 1933. $3

I MAY BE GONE FOR A LONG LONG TIME. Brown & Von Tilzer. 1917. $3

I ONLY FOUND YOU FOR SOMEBODY ELSE. Newman & Jones. 1932. $3

I ROSEWOOD SPINET. Tobias & Simon. 1948. $1

I SENT MY WIFE TO THE THOUSAND ISLANDS. Sterling Moran & Von Tilzer. 1916. $3

I WAKE UP SMILING. Leslie & Ahlert. 1933. $3

I WANT SOMEBODY TO CHEER ME UP. Kahn & Fiorito. 1925. $2

I WANT TO BE HAPPY. Harbach, Caesar & Youmans. 1924. $2

I WANT TO BE LOVED LIKE A BABY. William Witol. 1923. $2

I WANT TO BORROW A SWEET MAMA. Fred Fisher. 1922. $3

I WANT TO BRING YOU A RING. John Golden. 1910. $5

I WANT TO GO BACK TO MICHIGAN. Waterson, Berlin & Snyder. 1914. $3

I WANT TO GO TO TOKYO. McCarthy & Fisher. 1914. $3

I WAS IN THE MOOD. Pola & Carr. 1933. $2

I WENT OUT OF MY WAY. Helen Bliss. 1941. $1

I WENT TO YOUR WEDDING. L. Robinson. 1952. $1

I WISH I KNEW. Gordon & Warren. 1945. $1

I WISH I KNEW. Spencer, Anderson & Bryant. 1922. $2

I WISH THAT HE WAS BACK IN TIPPERARY. Brennan & Ball. 1915. $4

I WISH THAT I COULD HIDE INSIDE THIS LETTER. Tobias & Simon. 1943. $1

I WONDER WHAT'S BECOME OF SALLY. Yellen & Ager. 1945. $2

I WONDER WHERE MY BABY IS TO-NIGHT. Kahn & Donaldson. 1926. $2

I WOULDN'T STEAL THE SWEETHEART OF A SOLDIER BOY. Bryan & Paley. 1916. $2

I'D LIKE TO GIVE YOU SOMETHING THAT YOU'VE NEVER HAD BEFORE. Melville Collins. 1913. $6

I'D LIKE TO SEE SAMOA OF SAMOA. Bullock & Spina. 1937. $4

IF HE CAN FIGHT LIKE HE CAN LOVE, GOOD NIGHT GERMANY. Clarke, Rogers & Meyer. 1918. $3

IF I CAN'T HAVE YOU. Bryan & Meyer. 1929. $3

IF I HAD YOU. Shapiro, Campbell & Connelly. 1928. $3

IF I SHOULD LOSE YOU. Robin & Rainger, Cole Porter. 1935. $2

IF I WERE KING. Ingleton, Grey & Kornblum. 1926. $2

IF I WERE MOTHER EVE INSTEAD OF EVA. Melville Collins. 1913. $3

IF THEY EVER PUT A TAX ON LOVE. Ehrlich & Osborne. 1918. $3

IF WAR IS WHAT SHERMAN SAID IT WAS. Sterling & Gumble. 1915. $3

IF YOU PLEASE. Burke & Van Heusen. 1943. $1

IF YOU'RE IN LOVE YOU'LL WALTZ. McCarthy & Tierney. 1926. $2

IF YOU WANT THE RAINBOW. Rose & Dixon. 1928. $9

IF YOU'LL REMEMBER ME. Graff & Ball. 1908. $5

I'LL ALWAYS BE IN LOVE WITH YOU. Ruby, Green & Stept. 1929. $2

I'LL ALWAYS LOVE YOU. Livingston & Evans. 1950. $1

I'LL ALWAYS REMEMBER YOU. Klages & Greer. 1926. $3

I'LL BE HAPPY WHEN THE PREACHER MAKES YOU MINE. Lewis, Young & Donaldson. 1919. $2

I'LL BE SEEING YOU. Kahal & Fain. 1938. $1

I'LL ALWAYS LOVE YOU. Livingston & Evans. 1950. $1

I'LL ALWAYS REMEMBER YOU. Klages & Greer. 1926. $3

I'LL BE HAPPY WHEN THE PREACHER MAKES YOU MINE. Lewis, Young & Donaldson. 1919. $2

I'LL BE SEEING YOU. Kahal & Fain. 1938. $1

I'LL BUY THAT DREAM. Magidson & Wrubel. 1945. $1

I'LL CLOSE MY EYES. Cliff Friend. 1929. $1

I'LL FOLLOW YOU. Turk & Ahlert. 1932. $2

I'LL GET BY. Turk & Ahlert. 1928. $3

I'LL LOVE YOU MORE FOR LOSING YOU AWHILE. Egan & Whiting. 1918. $3

I'LL NEVER HAVE ANOTHER PAL LIKE MARY MINE. Oppenheim & Cooper. 1911. $4

I'LL NEVER SMILE AGAIN. Ruth Lowe. 1939. $2

I'LL NEVER STOP LOVING YOU. Kahn & Brodszky. 1954. $1

I'LL SAY SHE DOES. DeSylva, Kahn & Jolson. 1918. $3

I'LL SEE YOU IN MY DREAMS. Kahn & Jones. 1924. $3

I'LL SING YOU A THOUSAND LOVE SONGS. Warner & Dubin. 1919. $2

I'LL STRING ALONG WITH YOU. Dubin & Warren. 1919. $2

I'LL TAKE YOU HOME AGAIN, KATHLEEN. Thomas P. Westendorf. 1932. $1

I'M A BIG GIRL NOW. Hoffman, Drake & Lovingston. 1946. $1

I'M A SENTIMENTAL DREAMER. Paskman & Kaufman. 1921. $2

I'M ALWAYS CHASING RAINBOWS. Elliott, Comstock & Gest. 1918. $2

I'M COMING BACK TO CALIFORNIA, THAT'S WHERE I BELONG. Brennan & Ball. 1916. $3

I'M FEATHERING MY NEST. Yellen & Ager. 1929. $2

I'M FOLLOWING YOU. Dreyer & MacDonald. 1929. $2

I'M FOREVER BLOWING BUBBLES. Brovin & Kellette. 1919. $2

I'M GLAD I CAN MAKE YOU CRY. McCarron & Morgan. 1918. $2

I'M GLAD I WAITED FOR YOU. Cahn & Styne. 1945. $1

I'M GLAD MY WIFE'S IN EUROPE. Johnson, Goetz & Goettler. 1914. $8

I'M GOING BACK TO CALIFORNIA. Brennan & Ball. 1916. $3

I'M GOING BACK TO CAROLINA. Downs & Erdman. 1913. $3

I'M GOING DOWN TO TENNESSE. Fields & Carroll. 1912. $3

I'M GOING HOME TO DIXIE. Dan Emmett. 1872. $25

I'M GOING ON THE WARPATH. Feist & Corin. 1907. $11

I'M GOING TO CLIMB THE BLUE RIDGE MOUNTAINS BACK TO YOU. Levenson & McConnell. 1919. $2

I'M GOING TO FIGHT MY WAY BACK TO CAROLINA. Baskette & Spiess. 1918. $6

I'M GOING TO SETTLE DOWN OUTSIDE OF LONDON TOWN WHEN I'M DRY, DRY, DRY. McCarthy & Fisher. 1919. $3

I'M HATIN' THIS WAITIN' AROUND. Tobias, Lewis & Mencher. 1937. $2

I'M IN A DANCING MOOD. Sigler, Gerhart & Hoffman. 1936. $3

I'M IN HEAVEN. Johnson, Hess & Ager. 1920. $2

I'M IN LOVE WITH YOU. Titsworth & Cowan. 1929. $2

I'M IN THE MARKET FOR YOU. McCarthy & Hanley. 1930. $2

I'M JUST A DANCING SWEETHEART. Tobias & Rose. 1931. $2

I'M JUST A LITTLE BLUE. Gillespie & Van Alstyne. 1922. $2

I'M JUST A LITTLE BOY BLUE. Washington & Young. 1934. $2

I'M JUST BEGINNING TO CARE. Seymour Simons. $2

I'M LAUGHING. McNamee & Zany. 1929. $2

I'M LOOKING FOR SOMEONE TO LOOK AFTER ME. Paskman, Parrish & Squires. 1925. $3

I'M LOOKING FORWARD TO GOIN' BACK HOME. Lewis Baer & Pokrass. 1934. $2

I'M MAKING BELIEVE. Gordon & Monaco. 1944. $1

I'M MAKIN' HAY IN THE MOONLIGHT. Seymour & Greer. 1932. $2

I'M MISSING THE KISSING OF SOMEONE. Davis & Bibo. 1926. $2

I'M MISUNDERSTOOD. Compton & Ricca. 1935. $2

I'M NEEDING YOU. Young & Little. 1930. $1

I'M ON A DIET OF LOVE. Gilbert & Baer. 1930. $2

I'M ON MY WAY TO DUBLIN BAY. Stanley Murphy. 1915. $4

I'M ON MY WAY TO MANDALAY. Bryan & Fisher. 1913. $2

I'M RUNNING AROUND IN CIRCLES TRYING TO SQUARE MYSELF WITH YOU. Baxter & Burnette. 1935. $2

I'M SITTING ON TOP OF THE WORLD. Young & Henderson. 1925. $2

I'M SORRY I'LL BE BUSY ALL NEXT WEEK. Gilroy & Linton. 1902. $6

I'M SORRY I MADE YOU CRY. N. J. Clesi. 1918. $2

I'M STEPPING OUT WITH A MEMORY TONIGHT. Magidson & Wrubel. 1940. $1

I'M STILL CARING. Vallee & Klenner. 1929. $2

I'M THE ONE WHO LOVES YOU. Grey & Kortlander. 1937. $1

I'M TIRED OF EVERYTHING BUT YOU. Isham Jones. 1925. $2

I'M TRYING SO HARD TO FORGET YOU. Chas. K. Harris. 1904. $4

I'M WALKING AROUND IN A DREAM. Lewis, Yoell & Spencer. 1929. $3

I'M WALKING BEHIND YOU. Billy Reid. 1943. $1

I'M YOURS. Harburg & Green. 1930. $2

IMPERIAL GUARD. John Philip Sousa. 1902. $3

I MUST BE SINGING, SINGING. Walters & Taubert. 1850. $35

IN A LITTLE GYPSY TEA ROOM. Leslie & Burke. 1925. $2

IN A SHADY LITTLE DELL IN DELAWARE. MacDonald & Carroll. 1914. $3

IN A LOVE BOAT WITH YOU. Atteridge, Romberg & Schwartz. 1919. $3

IN BLUEBIRD LAND. Albert Short. 1921. $1

IN MY ARMS. Loesser & Grouva. 1944. $1

IN MY GARDEN. Firestone & O'Keefe. 1929. $1

IN MY GONDOLA. Green & Warren. 1926. $1

IN REVOLUTIONARY MEXICO. Weinberg & Claypoole. 1914. $2

IN SECRET SERVICE I WON HER HEART. Bryan & Spencer. 1919. $1

IN THE CHAPEL IN THE MOONLIGHT. Billy Hill. 1936. $1

IN THE CITY OF BROKEN HEARTS. Edgar Allen. 1916. $2

IN THE GLOAMING, MOTHER DARLING. Potter & Whitmore. 1918. $1

IN THE GOLD FIELDS OF NEVADA. Leslie & Gottler. 1915. $2

IN THE HEART OF A ROSE. Walsh & DeCarme. 1912. $6

IN THE HEART OF THE KENTUCKY HILLS. Gilbert & Muir. 1913. $3

IN THE LAND OF THE BUFFALO. Williams & Van Alstyne. 1907. $4

IN THE LAND WHERE THE SHAMROCK GROWS. Beardsley & Schwartz. 1919. $2

IN THE MOONLIGHT. Kalmar & Ruby. 1932. $2

IN THE SHADE OF THE CATHEDRAL. Ferd Rossmark. 1898. $15

IN THE SHADE OF THE OLD APPLE TREE. Williams & Van Alstyne. 1905. $7

IN THE VALLEY OF THE MOON. Jeff Branen. 1913. $4

INDIANA. MacDonald & Hanley. 1917. $3

INDIANA POLKA. Edmund Jaeger. 1866. $16

INDIANOLA. Henry & Onivas. 1918. $2

(AN) INNOCENT AFFAIR. Walter Kent. 1939. $2

INTERMEZZO. Heinz Provost. 1936. $2

IRELAND MUST BE HEAVEN FOR MY MOTHER CAME FROM THERE. McCarthy, Johnson & Fisher, 1916. $2

(THE) IRISHMAN'S SHANTY. Matt Peel. 1859. $27

IRENE. McCarthy & Tierney. 1919. $2

ISADORA. Jarre & Black. 1968. $1

IS EVERYBODY HAPPY? F. Williams. 1905. $4

IS SHE MY GIRL FRIEND. Yellen & Ager. 1927. $3

ISN'T THAT JUST LIKE LOVE? Burke & Van Heusen. 1940. $1

IT CAN'T BE WRONG. Gannon & Steiner. 1942. $2

IT COULD HAPPEN TO YOU. Burke & Van Heusen. 1944. $1

IT HAPPENED IN MONTEREY. Rose & Wayne. 1930. $1

IT HAPPENS EV'RY TIME. Bobby Worth. 1942. $1

IT MIGHT AS WELL BE SPRING. Rodgers & Hammerstein. 1945. $1

IT MUST BE TRUE. Arnheim & Clifford. 1930. $1

IT MUST BE YOU. Rogers & Gumble. 1922. $2

IT'S A HABIT OF MINE. Robin & Whiting. 1929. $3

IT'S A HAP-HAP-HAPPY DAY. Neiberg, Timberg & Shaples. 1939. $2

IT'S ALL MY FAULT. Flynn, Meyer & Wendling. 1932. $2

IT'S A LONG WAY BACK TO HOME, SWEET HOME. Jones & Albert. 1910. $3

IT'S A LONG WAY TO BERLIN. Fields & Flatow. 1917. $2

IT'S EASY TO FALL IN LOVE. Goetz & Wendling. 1930. $2

IT'S GREAT TO BE A SOLDIER MAN. Drisland & Morse. 1907. $6

IT'S NEVER MERRY XMAS WHEN YOU ARE FAR FROM HOME. Clinton & Jones. 1915. $3

IT'S NEVER TOO LATE TO BE SORRY. Dempsey & Burke. 1915. $2

IT'S THE DREAMER IN ME. Dorsey & Van Heusen. 1938. $1

IT'S WAY PAST MY DREAMING TIME. Newman, Samuels & Vallee. 1939. $1

I'VE FOUND MY LOVE. Ainslow & Allsorn. 1946. $1

I'VE GOT A FEELING I'M FALLING. Rose, Link & Waller. 1929. $3

I'VE GOT AN INVITATION TO A DANCE. Symes, Neiburg & Levenson. 1934. $2

I'VE GOT RINGS ON MY FINGERS. Maud Lambert. 1909. $3

I'VE GOT TO SING A TORCH SONG. Dubin & Warren. 1933. $2

I'VE GOT YOU UNDER MY SKIN. Cole Porter. 1936. $2

I'VE HAD MY MOMENTS. Kahn & Donaldson. 1934. $2

I'VE HEARD THAT SONG BEFORE. Styne & Cahn. 1942. $1

I'VE LOST MY HEART. Henry & Hamilton. 1931. $2

I'VE NEVER HAD A SWEETHEART LIKE YOU. Wever & Mann. 1937. $2

I'VE TOLD EVERY LITTLE STAR. Hammerstein & Kern. 1932. $2

I'VE WAITED A LIFETIME FOR YOU. Goodwin & Edwards. 1929. $1

JA-DA. Bob Darleton. 1918. $5

JEALOUS. Malie & Finch. 1924. $4

JEANIE MORRISON. Motherwell & Dempster. 1843. $25

JEANNINE, I DREAM OF LILAC TIME. Gilbert & Shilkret. 1928. $2

JEEPERS CREEPERS. Mercer & Warren. 1938. $2

JENNY GET YOUR HOE CAKE DONE. J. W. Sweeney, Frith & Hale. 1840. $35

JENNY LIND'S LAST NIGHT IN ENGLAND. Wm. Jeffreys. Date unknown. $20

JERICHO. Robin & Myers. 1929. $2

JERRY. O'Neil & Baskette. 1919. $2

JERRY MON CHERI. Murphy & Tierney. 1918. $2

JINGLE, JINGLE, JINGLE. Burkhardt & Franklin. 1910. $4

JOAN OF ARC. Roden & Kendis. 1916. $6

JOAN OF ARC THEY ARE CALLING YOU. Bryan, Weston & Wells. 1917. $3

JOANNE. Robertson, Persell & Smith. 1925. $2

JOCKEY HAT AND FEATHER. Julia & Brodwig. 1860. $22

JOHNNY GET YOUR GUN AND BE A SOLDIER. Yellen & Glogau. 1917. $8

JOHNNY ZERO. David & Lawnhurst. 1943. $1

JOOBALAI. Robin & Rainger. 1938. $2

JOSEPHINE. Kahn. 1927. $1

JUNE NIGHT. Baer & Friend. 1922. $1

JUST A BABY'S PRAYER AT TWILIGHT. Lewis, Young & Jerome. 1918. $2

JUST A BIRD'S EYE VIEW. Kahn & Donaldson. 1926. $1

JUST A COTTAGE SMALL BY A WATERFALL. De Sylva & Hanley. 1925. $2

JUST A GIGOLO. Casuci & Caesar. 1929. $2

JUST A GIRL THAT MEN FORGET. Dubin, Rath & Carren. 1923. $1

JUST A LITTLE CLOSER. Johnson & Meyer. 1930. $1

JUST A LITTLE ROCKING CHAIR AND YOU. Fitzgibbon, Drislane & Morse. 1905. $6

JUST A LITTLE SPRAY OF ROSES. Merrill & Dinsmore. 1910. $2

JUST A MEMORY. DeSylva, Brown & Henderson. 1927. $2

JUST A PRAYER AWAY. Tobias & Kapp. 1944. $1

JUST A WORD OF SYMPATHY. Kahn & Van Alstyne. 1916. $2

JUST ACROSS THE BRIDGE OF GOLD. Sterling & Von Tilzer. 1905. $3

JUST AN ECHO IN THE VALLEY. Woods, Campbell & Connelly. 1932. $2

JUST ANOTHER DAY WASTED AWAY. Tobias & Turk. 1927. $1

JUST AS YOUR MOTHER WAS. Sterling & Von Tilzer. 1917. $1

JUST BECAUSE IT REMINDS ME OF YOU. Parkins & Norton. 1906. $3

JUST BECAUSE YOU'RE YOU. Turk & Robinson. 1922. $2

JUST ENOUGH SPICE. James White. 1914. $5

JUST FOR THE SAKE OF YOUR MOTHER. Schaeffer & Leventhal. 1917. $5

JUST FRIENDS. Lewis & Klenner. 1931. $1

JUST LIKE A MELODY OUT OF THE SKY. Walter Donaldson. 1929. $1

JUST LIKE A RAINBOW. Eral & Fiorito. 1921. $1

JUST LIKE WASHINGTON CROSSED THE DELAWARE, PERSHING WILL CROSS THE RHINE. Johnson & Meyer. 1918. $2

JUST TRY TO PICTURE ME BACK HOME IN TENNESSEE. Jerome & Donaldson. 1915. $1

JUST YOU, JUST ME. Klages, & Greer. 1929. $2

KAISER BILL. Haller & Beatty. 1917. $2

KARAMA. Mabel McKinley. 1904. $5

KEEP ON THE SUNNY SIDE. Drislane & Morse. 1906. $3

KENTUCKY BLUES. Clarence Gaskill. 1921. $2

KERRY MILLS BARN DANCE. Kerry Mills. 1908. $10

KINDA PECULIAR BROWN. Burke & Van Heusen. 1943. $1

KIND OF A DRAG. Jimmy Harris. 1966. $1

(A) KISS IN THE DARK. Herbert & DeSylva. 1922. $3

KISS ME GOODNIGHT, NOT GOODBYE. Furthman & Hanley. 1931. $2

KISS WALTZ. Dubin & Burke. 1930. $2

KITTY TYRELL. Jeffreys & Clover. 1850. $45

K-K-KATY. Geoffrey O'Hara. 1918. $2

KNITTING. Bruce & Alioto. 1915. $2

LA FILLE DU REGIMENT. Donisetti. 1850. $30

LA VEEDA. Cincent & Alden. 1920. $4

LADDIE BOY. Cobb & Edwards. 1917. $2

LADY ANGELINE. Reed & Christie. 1912. $3

(THE) LADY IN RED. Dixie & Wrubel. 1935. $2

(THE) LADY WITH THE AUBURN HAIR. Sterling & Dreyfus. 1888. $3

LAFF IT OFF. Kalmar & Ruby. 1924. $3

LAMBETH WALK. Gay, Furber & Rose. 1937. $2

(THE) LAMENT OF THE IRISH IMMIGRANT. Wm. Dempster & Wm. Blackwood. 1842. $28

(THE) LAMP ON THE CORNER. Washington & Lara. 1938. $2

(THE) LAND OF MAKE BELIEVE. Freeman. 1919. $2

(THE) LANGUAGE OF LOVE. Lawrence & Pokrass. 1937. $2

LAST NIGHT WAS THE END OF THE WORLD. Sterling & Von Tilzer. 1912. $3

(THE) LAST ROUNDUP. Billy Hill. 1933. $2

LAST YEAR'S GIRL. Swanstrom & Alter. 1933. $2

LAUGH CLOWN LAUGH. Lewis, Young & Fiorito. 1928. $3

LAUGHING IRISH EYES. Mitchell & Stept. 1936. $3

LAY ME DOWN AND SAVE THE FLAG. Root & Paulina. 1864. $25

LAZY LOU'SIANA MOON. Walter Donaldson. 1930. $1

LEARNING. Symes, Neiburg & Levinson. 1934. $2

LET ME HAVE MY DREAMS. Calroke & Akst. 1929. $3

LET ME SEE YOUR RAINBOW SMILE. Havez & Barron. 1913. $2

LET THE REST OF THE WORLD GO BY. Brennan & Ball. 1919. $2

(THE) LETTER THAT NEVER CAME. Dresser & Sturm. 1887. $7

LET'S ALL BE AMERICANS NOW. Berlin, Leslie & Meyer. 1917. $3

LET'S ALL BE GOOD PALS TOGETHER. Davis & Erfman. 1919. $2

LET'S BRING NEW GLORY TO OLD GLORY. Gordon & Warren. 1942. $1

LET'S FALL IN LOVE. Koehler & Arlen. 1933. $2

LET'S GET FRIENDLY. Yellen, Silvers & Dougherty. 1931. $1

LET'S GET LOST. Loesser & McHugh. 1943. $1

LET'S GIVE THREE CHEERS FOR LOVE. Gordon & Revel. 1934. $2

LET'S GO INTO A PICTURE SHOW. McRee & Von Tilzer. 1908. $8

LET'S GO TO SAVANNAH, GA. Muir, Gilbert & Abrahams. 1912. $4

LET'S PUT OUT THE LIGHTS AND GO TO SLEEP. Hupfeld. 1932. $1

LET'S TAKE THE LONG WAY HOME. Mercer & Arlen. 1944. $2

LET'S TODDLE. Goetz, Clarke & Grant. 1914. $3

L-I-B-E-R-T-Y Ted Barroh. 1916. $2

LIBERTY BELL. Mohr & Goodwin. 1917. $3

LIEBESTRAUM. Franz Liszt. 1935. $1

LIGHT HEARTED MARCH. J. E. Magruder. 1877. $15

LIKE A BREATH OF SPRINGTIME. Dubin & Burke. 1929. $2

LIKE AN ANGEL YOU FLEW INTO EVERYONE'S HEART. Stone, McLaughlin & Mills. 1927. $4

LIKE ME A LITTLE BIT LESS. Adamson & Lane. 1933. $2

LINDA. Jack Lawrence. 1946. $1

LINGER AWHILE. Rose & Owens. 1923. $2

LITTLE ANNIE ROONEY. Michael Nolan. 1890. $15

(A) LITTLE BIRCH CANOE AND YOU. Roberts & Callagan. 1918. $3

(A) LITTLE BIRD TOLD ME. Harvey Brooks. 1948. $1

(A) LITTLE BIT OF SUNSHINE. MacDonald, Goodwin & Hanley. 1918. $1

(A) LITTLE BOY CALLED "TAPS". Madden & Morse. 1904. $5

(A) LITTLE CHURCH AROUND THE CORNER. Walker & Burke. 1934. $1

LITTLE CRUMBS OF HAPPINESS. Ball & Brennan. 1920. $2

(THE) LITTLE FORD RAMBLED RIGHT ALONG. Foster & Gay. 1914. $3

(THE) LITTLE GRAY MOTHER WHO WAITS ALL ALONE. Grossman & DeCosta. 1915. $2

LITTLE GREEN APPLES. Bobby Russell. 1968. $1

(THE) LITTLE HOUSE THAT LOVE BUILT. Lam & Blanke. 1905. $2

LITTLE JAPANESE DOLL. Graff & Hart. 1922. $3

LITTLE LADY MAKE BELIEVE. Tobias & Simon. 1938. $2

LITTLE LANE. Penaloza & Filberto. 1933. $2

LITTLE MOTH KEEP AWAY FROM THE FLAMES. Costello & Von Tilzer. 1924. $2

LITTLE MOTHER. Rapee & Pollack. 1928. $3

(THE) LITTLE OLD CHURCH IN THE VALLEY. Kahn, Arnold & Van Alstyne. 1931. $2

LITTLE OLD CROSSROAD STORE. Mercer & Tinturin. 1932. $2

LITTLE OLD LADY. Carmichael & Adams. 1936. $2

(THE) LITTLE OLD MILL. Pelosi, Ilda & Towers. 1947. $1

(A) LITTLE ON THE LONELY SIDE. Robertson, Weldon & Cananaugh. 1944. $1

LITTLE PAL. Jolson. 1929. $5

(THE) LITTLE SHOW. Dietz & Schwartz. 1929. $1

LITTLE SKIPPER. Nick & Chas. Kenny. 1939. $1

LITTLE TOWN IN THE OULD COUNTY DOWN. Pascoe, Carlo & Sanders. 1921. $1

LIVING A LIFE OF DREAMS. Rubey Cowan. 1930. $2

LIZZIE. Heebner. 1905. $5

LOADING UP THE MANDY LEE. Murphy & Marshall. 1915. $1

LOG CABIN SONG. Alexander Kile. 1840. $50

LONELINESS. Pollack & Clare. 1928. $1

LONELINESS. Washington & Young. 1948. $1

LONELY HEART. Irene Wicker. 1936. $8

LONELY LANE. Fain & Kahal. 1933. $1

LONESOME AND SORRY. Davis & Conrad. 1926. $2

LONG AGO. Kern & Gershwin. 1938. $2

LONG BOY. Herschell, Walker & Williams. 1917. $2

LOOK FOR THE SILVER LINING. Bolton, Grey & Kern. 1920. $2

LOOK WHAT YOU'VE DONE. Kalmar & Ruby. 1932. $3

LOOKING AT THE WORLD. Malie & Steiger. 1926. $1

LOOP DE LOOP. Vann & Dong. 1962. $1

LORRAINE. Bryan & Fisher. 1917. $2

LOSING YOU. Cliff Friend. 1927. $1

LOST. Davis & Hanley. 1922. $3

LOST. Ohman, Mercer & Teeter. 1936. $1

LOUISE. Robin & Whiting. 1939. $2

LOU'SIANA LULLABY. Zoeller & Bernhard. 1928. $1

(THE) LOUSLINE POLKA. Chas. D'Albert. 1860. $27

LOVABLE. Kahn & Woods. 1932. $2

LOVE AMONG THE MILLIONAIRES. Gilbert & Baer. 1930. $1

LOVE AMONG THE ROSES. Delehany & Catlin. 1869. $52

LOVE BIRD. Earl & Fiorito. 1921. $2

LOVE HAS A WAY. Schertzinger. 1924. $2

LOVE IS ALL. Tobias & Tomlin. 1940. $2

LOVE IS BLUE. Blackburn & Popp. 1968. $1

LOVE MAKES THE WORLD A MERRY-GO-ROUND. Lauder, Montague & De Pace. 1923. $2

LOVE IS JUST AROUND THE CORNER. Robin & Gensler. 1934. $1

LOVE IS LIKE A ROSE. Bryan & Meyer. 1929. $2

LOVE IS LIKE THAT. Benne Russell. 1931. $1

LOVE ME FOREVER. Kahn & Schertzinger. 1935. $2

LOVE SOMEBODY. Whitney & Kramer. 1948. $1

(A) LOVE STORY—INTERMEZZO. Henning & Provost. 1940. $2

LOVE TALES. Ryan & Rose. 1923. $2

LOVE WALKED IN. George & Ira Gershwin. 1938. $1

LOVELIGHT IN THE STARLIGHT. Freed & Hollander. 1938. $1

LOVELY LADY. Wood, Stamper & Levey. 1927. $2

LOVELY TO LOOK AT. Fields, McHugh & Kern. 1935. $2

(A) LOVELY WAY TO SPEND AN EVENING. Adamson & McHugh. 1943. $2

LOVER COME BACK TO ME. Romberg, Mandel & Hammerstein. 1928. $2

LOVERS LANE IS A LONESOME TRAIL. Loos & Lewis. 1923. $3

LOVE'S LITTLE JOURNEY. Peck & Wenrich. 1920. $2

LOVE'S LITTLE MARY BROWN. Davis & Greer. 1931. $2

LOVE'S OWN KISS. Friml & Harbach. 1913. $2

LOVEY MOON. Duggan & Lawrence. 1913. $3

LOVING. Manuel Klein. 1910. $4

LOYALTY IS THE WORD TODAY. Cahill & Andine. 1917. $2

LUCKY MOON. Branen & Stevens. 1909. $2

LULL ME TO SLEEP. Barron & Kerr. 1914. $2

LULLABY LANE. Wood & DeCosta. 1925. $4

LULLABY OF BROADWAY. Dubin & Warren. 1935. $2

LULLABY OF THE LEAVES. Young & Petkere. 1932. $1

LYING IN THE HAY. Franc-Nohain, Mirielle, Roberts & Pepper. 1932. $2

MAD ABOUT HIM. Clare & Conrad. 1921. $2

MAD ABOUT HIM, SAD WITHOUT HIM, HOW CAN I BE GLAD WITHOUT HIM BLUES. Markes & Charles. 1942. $1

MAIN STREET. Comden, Green & Edens. 1940. $2

MAIRZY DOATS. Drake, Hoffman & Livingston. 1943. $1

MAKE A WISH. Alter, Webster & Straus. 1937. $2

MAKE BELIEVE. Hammerstein & Kern. 1927. $2

MAKING EYES. Sterling & Von Tilzer. 1905. $5

MAMMY LAND. Nomis & Dixon. 1921. $2

MAMMY'S CHOCOLATE SOLDIER. Mitchell & Gottler. 1918. $3

MAMMY'S LITTLE COAL BLACK ROSE. Whiting & Egan. 1916. $2

MAMMY'S LULLABY. Lee Roberts. 1918. $8

MAMSELLE. Gordon & Goulding. 1947. $1

(A) MAN—A MAID. Straus, Stamper, Kay & Thompson. 1929. $3

MANDY AND ME. McKenna & Guble. 1918. $3

MANDY 'N ME. Kalmar, Conrad & Motzan. 1921. $2

MANDY LANE. Wm. McKenna. 1908. $3

MARCHING ALONG TOGETHER. Pola, Steinger & Dixon. 1932. $5

MARCHING THROUGH GEORGIA. H.C. Work. 1865. $35

MARGIE. Davis, Conrad & Robinson. 1920. $1

MARIA ELENA. Barcelata & Russell. 1933. $1

MARINA. Maxwell & Granata. 1959. $1

MARY ANN. Davis & Silver. 1927. $1

MARY LOU. Lyman, Waggner & Robinson. 1927. $2

MASSA'S IN DE COLD, COLD GROUND. Stephen Foster. 1850. $35

MAY I. Gordon & Revel. 1934. $6

MAYBE IT'S LOVE. Mitchell, Gottler & Meyer. 1930. $2

MARIE. Irving Berlin. 1928. $2

MARJORIE. Seaford & Simpson. 1908. $2

MARY HAD A LITTLE LAMB. Symes & Malne. 1936. $2

MARY PICKFORD. Sosman & Fairman. 1913. $6

MASQUERADE IN MEXICO. Raleigh & Wayne. 1945. $1

MAY TIME. DeSylva & Rose. 1924. $2

(THE) MEANING OF USA. Raymond Browne. 1912. $3

MEET ME SWEET KATHLEEN IN HONEYSUCKLE TIME. Helf & Roden. 1906. $2

MEET ME TONIGHT DEAR OLD PAL OF MINE. Martha Boswell. 1932. $2

MELLOW MOON. Wendell W. Hall. 1922. $1

MELODY IN F. A. Rubenstein. 1935. $1

MELODY FARM. Kahn, Kaper & Turmann. 1937. $1

MEMORIES. Kahn & Van Alstyne. 1915. $2

MEM'RIES OF ONE SWEET KISS. Jolson & Dreyer. 1929. $2

(THE) MERRY WIDOW WALTZ. Franz Lehar. 1908. $5

MICKEY. Williams & Moret. 1917. $2

MID THE SUNNY FIELDS OF DIXIE. Emily Smith. 1911. $3

MIGHTY LAK A ROSE. Stanton & Nevin. 1901. $8

MILKMAN KEEP THOSE BOTTLES QUIET. Raye & DePaul. 1944. $2

MINDIN' MY BUSINESS. Kahn & Donaldson. 1923. $2

MINE. DeSylva & Hanley. 1927. $1

MINE—ALL MINE. Ruby, Cowan & Stept. 1927. $1

(THE) MISSISSIPPI BUBBLE. Chauncey Haines. 1902. $3

MISSISSIPPI DREAM BOAT. Brown, Freed & Fain. 1943. $1

MISSISSIPPI MOON. Gunsky & Goldstein. 1922. $2

MISTER MOVING PICTURE MAN. Moriarty & Shannon. 1912. $3

MODULATIONS. Clarence M. Jones. 1923. $1

MOLLY MOLLOY. Thompson & Rycroft. 1901. $2

MONSIEUR BABY. Robin & Rainger. 1933. $3

MONTANA. Byrd & Weeks. 1921. $

MOON ABOUT TOWN. Duke, Harburg, Swanstrom, Alter & Pokrass. 1933. $2

(THE) MOON GOT IN MY EYES. Burke & Johnston. 1937. $1

(THE) MOON IS IN TEARS TONIGHT. Scholl & Jerome. 1937. $1

(THE) MOON IS LOW. Freed & Brown. 1929. $2

(THE) MOON OF MANAKOORA. Loesser & Newman. 1937. $2

MOON SONG THAT WASN'T FOR ME. Coslow & Johnston. 1932. $2

MOONLIGHT AND ROSES. Lemare, Black & Moret. 1925. $2

MOONLIGHT AND SHADOWS. Robin & Hollander. 1936. $2

MOONLIGHT BAY. Madden & Wenrich. 1912. $3

MOONLIGHT BECOMES YOU. Burke & Van Heusen. 1942. $1

MOONLIGHT MADNESS. Davis & Coots. 1928. $

MOONLIGHT ON THE DANUBE. Byron Gay. 1925. $2

MOONLIGHT SAVING TIME. Kahal & Richman. 1931. $1

MORNING WILL COME. Jolson, DeSylva & Conrad. 1923. $5

M-O-T-H-E-R. Johnson & Morse. 1915. $2

M-O-T-H-E-R A WORD THAT MEANS THE WORLD TO ME. Johnson & Morse. 1915. $2

MOTHER I'LL COME BACK A BETTER BOY. Armstrong & Klickman. 1919. $3

MOVING DAY. Sterling & Von Tilzer. 1906. $3

MUDDY WATER. Trent, DeRose & Richman. 1926. $1

MUSIC BOX RAG. Lucky Roberts. 1914. $5

MUSIC MAESTRO, PLEASE. Magidson & Wrubel. 1938. $1

(THE) MUSIC STOPPED. Adamson & McHugh. 1943. $2

MUTILATION RAG. Zema Randale. 1915. $

MY ADOBE HACIENDA. Massey & Penny. 1941. $1

MY BEAUTIFUL LADY. McClellan & Caryll. 1911. $6

MY BEST GIRL. Walter Donaldson. 1924. $

MY BLUE HEAVEN. Donaldson & Whiting. 1927. $1

MY CONFESSION. Bob Wills. 1942. $1

MY CREOLE SUE. Gussie L. Davis. 1898. $12

MY CROSS-EYED GIRL. Long & Autry. 1935. $2

MY DARLING. Heyman & Myers. 1932. $1

MY DARLING, MY DARLING, Frank Loesser. 1948. $1

MY FIRST LOVE TO LAST. Marion & Whiting. 1933. $3

MY GEE GEE FROM THE FIJI ISLES. Brown & Von Tilzer. 1920. $2

MY GIRL FROM THE USA. Freedman & McConnell. 1918. $3

MY HAPPINESS. Peterson & Bergantine. 1933. $1

MY HAWAIIAN MELODY. Ringle & Coots. 1921. $2

MY HAWAIIAN SUNSHINE. Gilbert & Morgan. 1916. $1

MY HEART'S TONIGHT IN TEXAS. Roder & Witt. 1900. $11

MY HEART'S DESIRE. Marion & Whiting. 1933. $2

MY HOME IN THE GOLDEN WEST. Evangeline Green. 1918. $2

MY LITTLE GIRL. Lewis, Dillon & Von Tilzer. 1915. $6

MY LOTUS FLOWER. Selden & Furth. 1907. $5

MY LOVE FOR YOU. Gus & Grace Kahn. 1930. $2

MY MAMA'S WITH THE ANGELS. Little & Little. 1905. $8

MY MOTHER'S EYES. Gilbert & Baer. 1928. $2

MY OLD KENTUCKY HOME. Stephen Foster. 1903. $12

MY PRETTY FIREFLY. Murphy, Glogau & Piantadosi. 1915. $3

MY RIVER HOME. Young & Petkere. 1932. $2

MY RUBY BELLE. Gerard & Armstrong. 1904. $10

MY SISTER AND I. Zaret, Whitney & Kramer. 1941. $

MY SONG OF THE NILE. Bryan & Meyer. 1929. $2

MY SUMURUM GIRL. Jolson & Hirsch. 1912. $4

MY SUNNY SUE. Sterling & Hamilton. 1902. $7

MY SWEETER THAN SWEET. Marion & Whiting. 1929. $3

MY SWEETHEART. Gillespie & Shay. 1924. $1

MY SWEETIE WENT AWAY. Turk & Handman. 1923. $

MY TEXAS ROSE. Davies & Keating. 1915. $3

MY WALKING STICK. Irving Berlin. 1938. $2

MY WHOLE DAY IS SPOILED. Young, Newman & Monaco. 1934. $1

MY YANKEE BOY. Grossman, Frisch & Solman. 1917. $2

'N' EVERYTHING. DeSylva, Kahn & Jolson. 1918. $3

NAJO. O'Neil, Wiedoeft & Holliday. 1921. $2

(THE) NAVY WILL BRING THEM BACK. Johnston & Shuster. 1918. $2

NEAL OF THE NAVY. Charles Bayha. 1915. $2

NEARNESS OF YOU. Donaldson, Washington & Carmichael. 1940. $1

NEAR YOU. Goell & Craig. 1947. $1

NEDRA WALTZES. Florence McPherran. 1906. $5

NEVER A DAY GOES BY. Donaldson, Rose & Parish. 1943. $2

(A) NEW MOON AND AN OLD SERENADE. Silver, Block & Coslow. 1939. $2

NEW YORK AIN'T NEW YORK ANYMORE. Rose, Brown & Henderson. 1925. $1

NIGHT AND DAY. Cole Porter. 1932. $2

(THE) NIGHT IS YOUNG AND YOU'RE SO BEAUTIFUL. Rose & Suesse. 1936. $2

(THE) NIGHT WE MET IN HONOMU. Lanny Ross. 1941. $1

NIGHT WIND. Rothberg & Pollock. Donaldson, Douglas & Gumble. 1934. $2

1915 RAG. Dent & Young. 1912. $17

NO MORE AT EVENING. Post & Nitke. 1919. $3

NO NO NORA. Fiorito & Kahn. 1922. $3

NO ONE ELSE CAN TAKE YOUR PLACE. Chas. K. Harris. 1913. $10

NOBODY BUT YOU. Magidson, Washington & Cleary. 1929. $3

NOBODY CARES IF I'M BLUE. Clarke & Akst. 1929. $3

NOBODY KNOWS AND NOBODY SEEMS TO CARE. Irving Berlin. 1919. $2

NOBODY KNOWS WHAT A RED HEAD MAMMA CAN DO. Mills, Dubin, Fain. 1924. $2

NOBODY LIED. Nerman, Berry & Weber. 1922. $5

NOW I LAY ME DOWN TO SLEEP. Fox & Walbridge. 1866. $25

NOW MOSES. Henry G. Work. 1865. $12

O KATHARINA. Gilbert & Fall. 1924. $3

O MISTER MAN UP IN THE MOON. Koehler & McHugh. 1936. $2

O SWIFT WE GO. Knight & Field. 1850. $35

OCEANA ROLL. Lewis & Dennis. 1911. $2

OF THEE I SING. Geo. & Ira Gershwin. 1931. $2

OGALALLA. Bryan & Snyder. 1909. $3

OH BOYS CARRY ME ALONG. Stephen Foster. 1851. $30

OH BY JINGO. Brown & Von Tilzer. 1919. $2

OH DADDY! PLEASE DADDY, COME HOME. Norrett & Dellon. 1926. $1

OH FRENCHY. Ehrlich & Conrad. 1918. $2

OH GOD, LET MY DREAM COME TRUE. Merritt & Piantadosi. 1916. $3

OH THAT TEASING MAN. Goodwin & Meyer. 1912. $3

OH! WHAT IT SEEMED TO BE. Benjamin, Weiss & Carle. 1945. $1

OH! YOU CAN'T FOOL AN OLD HOSS FLY. Frankly, Vincent & Von Tilzer. 1924. $3

OH YOU CIRCUS DAY. Lessing & Monaco. 1909. $4

OL' CAR'LINA. Cooke. 1920. $1

OLD APPLE TREE. J. Jerome. 1938. $2

(THE) OLD ARMCHAIR. Henry Russell. 1849. $22

(THE) OLD BACHELOR. Thos. H. Bayly. 1850. $27

OLD FOLKS AT HOME. Stephen Foster. 1851. $25

OLD GLORY. Franklin E. Hathaway. 1917. $2

OLD PIANO ROLL BLUES. C. Coban. 1950. $2

(THE) OLD SCHOHARIE RIVER. Schermerhorn & Hobart. 1915. $2

OLD SOLDIERS NEVER DIE. Tom Glazer. 1951. $1

OLD SOUTH. J. W. Turner. 1876. $12

OLD ZIP COON. Anonymous. 1834. $45

ON ELLIN'S BOSOM BLUSHED A ROSE. T.Z. Weisenthal. 1840. $20

ON MIAMI SHORE. Victor Jacobi. 1919. $3

ON MOBILE BAY. Jones & Daniels. 1910. $3

ON RANCH 101. MacDonald & Puck. 1914. $2

ON THE HOKO MOKO ISLE. Klein & Von Tilzer. 1916. $3

ON THE MISSISSIPPI. McDonald, Carroll & Fields. 1912. $3

ON THE OLD FALL RIVER LINE. J. Jerome. 1913. $11

ON THE OLD SEE SAW. Gardenier & Edwards. 1906. $3

ON THE ROAD THAT LEADS BACK TO HOME. Gitz Rice. 1918. $2

ON THE STEPS OF THE GREAT WHITE CAPITOL. Clarke, Leslie & Abrahams. 1914. $3

ONCE AGAIN. Howard, Kornblum & Myers. 1919. $3

ONE KISS. Romberg, Mandel & Hammerstein. 1928. $3

ONE NIGHT IN MONTE CARLO. Silver, Sherman & Lewis. 1935. $2

ONE TWO BUTTON YOUR SHOE. Burke & Johnston. 1938. $2

ONLY A MESSAGE FROM HOME SWEET HOME. Fleming & Florant. 1905. $3

ONLY FOREVER. Burke & Monaco. 1940. $1

OOH YOU MISER YOU! Lewis & Wendling. 1934. $2

OPEN UP THE GOLDEN GATES TO DIXIELAND. Yellen & Van Schenck. 1919. $2

ORANGE COLORED SKY. DeLugg & Stein. 1950. $1

ORCHIDS IN THE MOONLIGHT. Kahn, Eliscu & Youmans. 1933. $2

ORIENT. Plettle & Whitmore. 1920. $3

OUR BUNGALOW OF DREAMS. Malie, Newman & Verges. 1927. $1

OUT OF SIGHT, OUT OF MIND. Fields & Levant. 1935. $2

OUT OF THE EAST. Havez & Rosey. 1918. $1

OVER SOMEBODY ELSE'S SHOULDER. Sherman & Lewis. 1934. $1

OVER THE TOP. Lourine Kummer. 1917. $2

OVER THERE. Geo. M. Cohan. 1917. $25

OVERTURE PATRIOTIC. Richard Weaver. 1908. $5

PADDLE YOUR OWN CANOE. Madden & Morse. 1905. $2

PAGAN LOVE SONG. Freed & Brown. 1929. $2

PAGE MISS GLORY. Dubin & Warren. 1935. $4

PAINTING THE CLOUDS WITH SUNSHINE. Dubin & Burke. 1929. $2

(THE) PAL THAT I LOVED STOLE THE GAL THAT I LOVED. Pease & Nelson. 1924. $1

PAL OF MY CRADLE DAYS. Montgomery & Piantadosi. 1925. $2

PAPER DOLL. Johnny Black. 1912. $2

PARADISE. Clifford & Brown. 1931. $3

PARIS IN THE SPRING. Gordon & Revel. 1935. $3

PARISIENNE. Brown & Von Tilzer. 1912. $3

PATCHES. Roberts & Callahan. 1919. $2

PAUL REVERE. Goodwin & Mohr. 1918. $2

PAXINOSCE. Ella Dinslow Jones. 1905. $3

PEANUTS — A NUTTY RAG. Ethel Earnist. 1911. $16

PENNIES FROM HEAVEN. Burke & Johnston. 1936. $1

PENNY SERENADE. Hallifan & Weersma. 1938. $1

PEOPLE. Styne & Merrill. 1936. $2

(A) PERFECT DAY. Carrie Jacobs Bond. 1910. $4

PERHAPS SHE'S ON THE RAILROAD. F. Blume. 1870. $16

(THE) PESKY SARPENT. Oakes & Swan. 1840. $32

PICK ME UP AND LAY ME DOWN IN DEAR OLD DIXIELAND. Kalmar & Ruby. 1922. $2

PICKANINNY BLUES. Frost & Klickmann. 1919. $4

PINEY RIDGE. MacDonald & Mohr. 1915. $2

PINK ELEPHANTS. Dixon & Woods. 1932. $2

PLANTATION TUNES. Jack Mahoney. 1913. $5

PLEASE. Robin & Rainger. 1932. $2

PLEASE PARDON US WE'RE IN LOVE. Gordon & Revel. 1937. $2

POLLY. J. S. Zamecnik. 1926. $2

POOR BOY. Casey Kelly. 1972. $1

POOR LITTLE BUTTERFLY IS A FLY GIRL NOW. Lewis, Young, & Jerome. 1919. $3

POOR LITTLE RHODE ISLAND. Cahn & Styne. 1944. $1

POOR PUNCHINELLO. Lewis, Young & Pollack. 1929. $3

POPPA DON'T PREACH TO ME. Frank Loesser. 1942. $1

PRACTICE MAKES PERFECT. Roberts & Gold. 1940. $1

PRAISE THE LORD AND PASS THE AMMUNITION. Loesser. 1942. $1

(THE) PREACHER AND THE BEAR. Joe Arzonia. 1928. $2

PRECIOUS. Egan, Pasterbacki & Whiting. 1926. $2

(A) PRECIOUS LITTLE THING CALLED LOVE. Davis & Coots. 1928. $3

(A) PRETTY GIRL IS LIKE A MELODY. Irving Berlin. 1919. $4

PRIDE OF THE PRAIRIE. Breen & Botsfors. 1907. $3

PRISONER OF LOVE. Robin, Gaskill & Colombo. 1931. $2

PUT YOUR ARMS AROUND ME HONEY. McRee & Von Tilzer. 1937. $2

PUT YOUR HEAD ON MY SHOULDER. Paul Anka. 1958. $1

RADIANCE. Atteridge, Stanley & Goodman. 1922. $2

RAGAMUFFIN ROMEO. DeCosta & Wayne. 1930. $1

RAGGY MILITARY TUNE. Lewis, Bastker & Roberts. 1912. $17

RAGTIME LIZ. Carle & Aarons. 1898. $12

RAIN. Hill & DeRose. 1934. $1

RAINBOW. Russ Hamilton. 1957. $1

RAINBOW ON THE RIVER. Webster & Alter. 1939. $2

RAMBLING ROSE. McCarthy & Burke. 1948. $1

RAMONA. Gilbert & Wayne. 1927. $2

(THE) RED LANTERN. Fred Fisher, McCarthy & Fisher. 1919. $2

RED MOON. Traver, deMartini & Kortlander. 1922. $2

RED SAILS IN THE SUNSET. Kennedy & Williams. 1935. $1

(THE) RED, WHITE AND BLUE. Arthur & Hirsch. 1914. $3

REDSKIN. Kerr & Zamecnik. 1929. $2

REMEMBER. Irving Berlin. 1925. $2

REMEMBER MY FORGOTTON MAN. Dubin & Warren. 1933. $2

(A) RENDEZVOUS WITH A DREAM. Robin & Rainger. 1936. $2

REVENGE. Lewis & Young. 1928. $2

RIDE, TENDERFOOT, RIDE. Mercer & Whiting. 1938. $3

(THE) ROBIN'S RETURN. Leander Fisher. 1912. $3

(THE) ROCK BESIDE THE SEA. Charlie C. Converse. 1857. $16

ROCK-A-BYE MOON. Johnson. 1932. $2

ROCKIN' ON THE PORCH. Seymour & Wendling. 1934. $1

(THE) ROGUE SONG. Grey & Stothart. 1929. $3

ROLL ALONG PRAIRIE MOON. Firerite, MacPherson & Von Tilzer. 1935. $2

ROLL ON MISSOURI. MacDonald & Carroll. 1913. $2

ROLLIN' PLAINS. Samuels, Whitcup & Powell. 1937. $1

ROLLING ALONG. Brown & Akst. 1936. $1

ROMANY LOVE. Lamb & Zamecnid. 1922. $1

RO-RO-ROLLIN' ALONG. Moll, Richman & Menscher. 1929. $1

ROSALIE. Cole Porter. 1937. $1

ROSE BUSH. Faustina Hasse Hedges. 1859. $11

(THE) ROSE IN HER HAIR. Buvin & Warren. 1935. $2

ROSE OF MANDALAY. Koehler & Magine. 1928. $1

(THE) ROSE OF NO MAN'S LAND. Caddigan & Brennan. 1918. $2

(THE) ROSE OF THE MOUNTAIN TRAIL. Caddigan & Brennan. 1918. $5

ROSES IN DECEMBER. Magidson, Oakland & Jessel. 1937. $3

ROSES OF PICARDY. Weatherly & Wood. 1916. $5

ROW, ROW, ROW. Jerome & Monaco. 1912. $3

RUBY. Parish & Roemheld. 1954. $1

RUMBLE, RUMBLE, RUMBLE. Frank Loesser. 1947. $1

RUNAWAY JUNE. Harold Freeman. 1915. $2

RUN HOME AND TELL YOUR MOTHER. Irving Berlin. 1911. $2

SAILING DOWN THE RIVER IN THE MOONLIGHT MANDY AND I. Caddigan & Brennan. 1914. $2

SALLY OF MY DREAMS. William Kernell. 1928. $2

SALLY WON'T YOU COME BACK? Buck & Stamper. 1921. $2

SAMMY BOY. 1917. $2

SANTA FE. Williams & Van Alstyne. $2

SATIN DOLL. Mercer, Ellington & Strayhorn. 1958. $1

SAY A PRAYER FOR THE BOYS OUT THERE. Grossman & Marr. 1917. $2

SAY IT WHILE DANCING. Davis & Silver. 1922. $2

SAY IT WITH A SLAP. Eliot Daniel. 1947. $1

SAYS MY HEART. Leosser & Lane. 1938. $3

SEEIN'S BELIEVIN'. Ehrlich & Cohen. 1903. $5

SEND ME AWAY WITH A SMILE. Weslyn & Piantadosi. 1918. $2

SEND BACK DEAR DADDY TO ME. Sullivan, Tenney & Mastof. 1918. $2

SEPTEMBER SONG. Weill & Anderson. 1938. $1

SERENADE. Donnelly & Romberg. 1925. $2

77 SUNSET STRIP. David & Livingston. 1959. $2

SHARING. Davis & Coots. 1930. $1

SHE IS THE SUNSHINE OF VIRGINIA. MacDonald & Carroll. 1916. $3

SHE REMINDS ME OF YOU. Gordon & Revel. 1934. $3

SHE SLEEPS NEXT TO THE OLD OHIO RIVER. Lam & Soman. 1913. $4

SHELLS OF OCEAN. J. W. Lake & J. W. Cherry. $25

SHEPHERD BOY'S ECHO SONG. J. Albert Snow. 1882. $11

SHEPHERD OF THE AIR. C. Gaskill. 1933. $2

(THE) SHEPHERD'S SONG. Grey & Stothart. 1929. $3

SHINE ON HARVEST MOON. Norworth & Bayes. 1918. $5

SHOO-FLY PIE AND APPLE PAN DOWDY. Wood & Gallop. 1945. $1

SHOULD I. Freed & Brown. 1929. $3

SHOW ME THE WAY. Davis, Lewis & Ross. 1924. $3

SIBONEY. E. Lecuona. 1929. $2

SILVER MOON. Donnelly & Romberg. 1927. $2

SILVER SLEIGH BELLS. E. T. Paull. 1906. $4

SILVER THREADS AMONG THE GOLD. Rexford & Danks. 1901. $5

SINCE THEY'RE PLAYING HAWAIIAN TUNES IN DIXIE. Grossman, Winkle & Lange. 1917. $4

SING BABY SING. Yellen & Pollack. 1935. $2

SINGING A VAGABOND SONG. Richman, Burton & Messenheimer. 1930. $2

SINGING BIRD. Longbrake & Edwards. 1909. $3

SINGING IN THE RAIN. Freed & Brown. 1929. $2

SISTER SUSIE'S SEWING SHIRTS FOR SOLDIERS. Weston & Darewski. 1914. $2

SIT DOWN YOU'RE ROCKING THE BOAT. Clarke & Jerome. 1913. $3

SITTIN' IN A CORNER. Kahn & Meyer. 1923. $1

SLEEPY HEAD. Davis & Greer. 1926. $2

SLEEPY HEAD. Kahn & Donaldson. 1934. $3

SLEEPY HOLLOW MID THE PINES. Baer & Rosenberg. 1906. $6

SLEEPY VALLEY. Sterling & Hanley. 1929. $2

SLOW AND EASY. Williams & Spencer. 1919. $2

SLOWLY. Raksia & Goell. 1945. $3

(A) SMILE WILL GO A LONG LONG WAY. Davis & Akst. 1923. $1

SMOKE GETS IN YOUR EYES. Kern & Harbach. 1933. $1

SMOKY MOKES. Abe Olman. 1899. $20

SMOTHER ME WITH KISSES AND KILL ME WITH LOVE. Bryan & Carroll. 1914. $2

SNOOKEY OOKUMS. Irving Berlin. 1913. $3

SO BLUE. Brown & Henderson. 1927. $1

SO DO I. Burke & Johnston. 1936. $2

SO, GOOD NIGHT. Carter & Rosen. 1943. $2

SO LONG, MOTHER. Egan & Kahn. 1917. $2

SO THIS IS HEAVEN. Burke & Spina. 1935. $1

SO THIS IS VENICE. Clarke. Leslie & Warren. 1923. $3

SOFT LIGHTS AND SWEET MUSIC. Irving Berlin. 1931. $2

(A) SOLDIER'S ROSARY. Dempsey & Burke. 1919. $3

SOME BOY. Buck & Stampe. 1912. $6

SOME SUNNY DAY. Irving Berlin. 1922. $2

SOME SWEET DAY. Shilkret & Pollack. 1929. $3

SOMEBODY MIGHTY LIKE. Bryan & Ward. 1929. $3

SOMEBODY MISSES SOMEBODY'S KISSES. Davis & Prival. 1919. $3

SOMEBODY'S SWEETHEART. Price & Bafunno. 1919. $2

SOMEDAY. Jimmie Hodges. 1944. $1

SOMEDAY, SOMEWHERE. Pollack & Rapee. 1928. $2

SOMEDAY, I'LL MEET YOU AGAIN. Washington & Steiner. 1944. $2

SOME DAY WE'LL MEET AGAIN. Conrad & Magidson. 1936. $2

SOME ENCHANTED EVENING. Hammerstein & Rodgers. 1949. $1

SOME SUNDAY MORNING. Koehler, Jerome & Heindorf. 1945. $1

SOME SWEET DAY. Shilkret & Pollack. $2

SOMETIMES THE DREAM COMES TRUE. Grossmith & Ward. 1915. $2

SOMEWHERE. Chas. K. Harris. 1906. $7

SOMEWHERE IN FRANCE IS DADDY. Great Howard. 1917. $2

SOMEWHERE IN FRANCE IS THE LILY. Howard & Johnson. 1917. $2

SOMEWHERE IN HAWAII. C.J. & J.A. MacMeekin. 1918. $3

SOMEWHERE ON BROADWAY. Carroll & Murphy. 1917. $2

SONG BIRD. Gillespie & Alford. 1909. $3

(THE) SONG FROM MOULIN ROUGE. Auric & Engvick. 1953. $1

(THE) SONG I WROTE FOR YOU. Burk & Levenson. 1932. $1

(THE) SONG IS YOU. Hammerstein & Kern. 1932. $2

SONG OF DETROIT. Campbell & Goldkette. 1930. $7

SONG OF THE DAWN. Yellen & Ager. 1930. $2

(THE) SONG OF THE FERRIS WHEEL. Schleiffarth & Sturgis. 1893. $25

SONNY BOY. Jolson, DeSylva, Brown & Henderson. $2

SOON. Hart & Rodgers. 1935. $1

SOUTH WIND. Gannon & Wayne. 1942. $1

SPELLBOUND CONCERTO. Miklos Rozsa. 1946. $1

(A) STAR FELL OUT OF HEAVEN. Gordon & Revel. 1936. $1

STAR SPANGLED BANNER. Francis S. Key. $25

STARLIGHT. Young & Petkere. 1931. $1

STARLIGHT HELP ME FIND THE ONE I LOVE. Young & Petkere. 1931. $2

(THE) STARS AND STRIPES FOR YOU AND I. Lyle & Agbeel. 1909. $7

STARS IN MY EYES. Fields & Kreisler. 1936. $2

(THE) STARS LOOKED DOWN. Smith & Cray. 1942. $1

STAY AS SWEET AS YOU ARE. Gordon & Revel. 1934. $2

STOP BEATIN' ROUND THE MULBERRY BUSH. Reichner & Boland. 1938. $1

STOP! YOU'RE BREAKING MY HEART. Koehler & Lane. 1937. $3

STORM CLOUD. Redding & Koockogey. 1909. $2

STRAIGHT FROM THE SHOULDER RIGHT FROM THE HEART. Gordon & Revel. 1934. $1

STRANGE LOVE. Heyman & Rozsa. 1946. $1

(THE) SUN'S IN MY HEART. Freed & Baer. 1932. $2

SUNSHINE AND ROSES. Kahn & Van Alstyne. 1913. $3

SUEZ. Pancoast, Grofe & DeRose. 1922. $2

SUNDAY, MONDAY OR ALWAYS. Burke & Van Heusen. 1943. $1

SWANEE BUTTERFLY. Rose & Donaldson. 1925. $2

SWANEE RIVER ROSE. Davis & Braverman. 1924. $3

SUSIE ANNA. Jerome & Schwartz. 1904. $4

SWEET ALICE GRAY. Gerard & Gilbert. 1920. $2

SWEET CHILD. Whiting, Lewis & Simon. 1925. $2

SWEET DAFFODILS. Percy Wenrich. 1905. $2

SWEET DREAMS, SWEETHEART. Jerome & Koehler. 1944. $1

SWEET LEILANI. Harry Owens. 1937. $1

SWEET LITTLE CARABOO. Laska & Kelly. 1904. $2

SWEET MEATS. Percy Wenrich. 1907. $17

SWEET MISERY OF LOVE. Hill & Simons. 1936. $1

SWEET PAPA. Love & Stroube. 1924. $1

SWEET PATOOTIE SAL. Wm. Loveman. 1920. $2

SWEET VARSITY SUE. Tobias. 1937. $1

(THE) SWEETEST WALTZ OF ALL. Harrison & Rose. 1925. $2

SWEETHEART DARLIN'. Kahn & Stothart. 1933. $2

SWEETHEART, WE NEED EACH OTHER. McCarthy & Tierney. 1929. $2

(THE) SWORD OF BUNKER HILL. Bernard Covert. 1855. $20

TAINT NO USE. Magidson & Lane. 1936. $2

TAKE A NUMBER FROM ONE TO TEN. Gordon & Revel. 1934. $2

TAKE ME BACK TO MY BOOTS AND SADDLE. Samuels, Whitcup & Powell. 1934. $3

TAKE ME BACK TO MY OWN LITTLE HOME SWEET HOME. Harry Verona. 1903. $3

TAKE ME TO MY ALABAM'. Tobias & Dillon. 1916. $2

TAKES TWO TO MAKE A BARGAIN. Gordon & Revel. 1935. $2

TALKING THROUGH MY HEART. Robin & Rainger. 1936. $1

TALKING TO THE MOON. Little & Baskette. 1926. $1

(THE) TAPE AND THE CHAIN. Stewart & Bowen. 1911. $3

TEA LEAVES. Berk, Capano & Freedman. 1948. $1

TELL ME. Callahan & Kortlander. 1919. $4

TELL ME IF U WANT SOMEBODY ELSE. Austing, Bargare, Mann & Cowan. 1924. $2

TELL ME LITTLE GYPSY. Irving Berlin. 1920. $2

TELL ME TONIGHT. Eyton & Spoliansky. 1932. $3

TELL ME WHY YOU AND I SHOULD BE STRANGERS. Fisher & Holden. 1922. $2

TEMPTATION. Freed & Brown. 1933. $2

TENDER IS THE NIGHT. Adamson & Donaldson. 1935. $2

TEN-TEN-TENNESSEE. Young. 1923. $2

TERRY WITH HER BONNIE BLUE E'E. John E. Andrews. 1845. $32.

TESSIE. Will Anderson. 1902. $4

THANK YOU AMERICA. Turmann & Grossman. 1941. $2

THAT DEAR OLD BELL. J. P. Skelly. 1879. $15

THAT GRAND OLD GENTLEMAN. Cobb & Edwards. 1918. $2

THAT GUY FROM THE ISLE OF CAPRI. Abbott & Wimbraer. 1935. $1

THAT LITTLE DREAM GOT NOWHERE. Burke & Van Heusen. 1940. $1

THAT LUCKY OLD SUN. Gillespie & Smith. 1949. $1

THAT PECULIAR RAG. F. M. Fagan. 1910. $12

THAT WONDERFUL KID FROM MADRID. MacDonald & Osborne. 1919. $2

THAT SLY OLD GENTLEMAN. Burke & Monaco. 1939. $2

THAT'S FOR ME. Rodgers & Hammerstein. 1945. $1

THAT'S LIFE I GUESS. Lewis & Rose. 1936. $1

THAT'S MY MAMMY. Pease, Baer & Nelson. 1928. $2

THAT'S MY WEAKNESS NOW. Green & Stept. 1928. $6

THAT'S WHAT THE DAISY SAID. Gumm & Von Tilzer. 1903. $3

THAT'S WHY I LOVE YOU. Donaldson & Ash. 1926. $2

THAT'S YOU BABY. Conrad, Mitchell & Gottler. 1929. $3

THEM HILLBILLIES ARE MOUNTAIN WILLIAMS NOW. Cavanaugh, Mysels & Sanford. 1935. $2

THEN CAME THE RAIN. Tobias & Levant. 1939. $1

THERE ARE RIVERS TO CROSS. Adams & Henderson. 1942. $1

THERE GOES MY ATTRACTION. Beiburg, Levinson & Bunch. 1936. $1

THERE, I'VE SAID IT AGAIN. Evans & Mann. 1941. $1

THERE WILL NEVER BE ANOTHER YOU. Gordon & Warren. 1942. $1

THERE'LL BE NO SOUTH. Brown, Akst & Richman. 1936. $1

THERE'LL COME A TIME. King & Burtnett. 1918. $3

THERE'S A LITTLE BLUE STAR IN THE WINDOW. Armstrong & Klickman. 1918. $8

THERE'S A DIFFERENT YOU IN YOUR HEART. Kohal & Fain. 1934. $1

THERE'S A FELLA WAITING IN POUGHKEEPSIE. Mercer & Arlen. 1944. $1

THERE'S A GIRL THAT'S MEANT FOR ME. S. J. Stasny. 1914. $2

THERE'S A GIRL IN THE HEART OF MARYLAND. MacDonald & Carroll. 1913. $2

THERE'S A HEART IN VIRGINIA FOR YOU. Sterling & Lange. 1917. $2

THERE'S A QUAKER DOWN IN QUAKER TOWN. Berg & Sooman. 1916. $2

THERE'S A ROSE IN OLD ERIN THAT'S BLOOMING FOR ME. Callahan, Briese & Klickman. 1915. $2

THERE'S A RED-HAIRED GIRL ON BROADWAY. E. Stenson. 1918. $2

THERE'S A SMALL HOTEL. Rodgers & Hart. 1936. $1

THERE'S A RAINBOW 'ROUND MY SHOULDER. Jolson, Rose & Dreyer. 1928. $5

THERE'S A VACANT CHAIR IN EVERY HOME TONIGHT. Bryan & Breuer. 1917. $2

THERE'S DANGER IN YOUR EYES, CHERIE. Richman, Meskill & Wendling. 1929. $2

THERE'S EVERYTHING NICE ABOUT YOU. Bryan, Terker & Wendling. 1929. $2

THERE'S NO OTHER GIRL. Davis, Coots & Engel. 1931. $2

THERE'S NO YOU. Adair & Hopper. 1944. $1

THERE'S NOTHING LEFT TO DO BUT SAY GOODBYE. Newman & Jones. 1933. $2

THERE'S OCEANS OF LOVE BY THE BEAUTIFUL SEA. Little & Coots. 1932. $2

THERE'S ONE CALIFORNIA FOR MINE. Bryan & Paley. 1915. $2

THERE'S RAIN IN MY EYES. Ager, McCarthy & Schwartz. 1938. $1

THERE'S REST FOR ALL IN HEAVEN. Johnston & Parkhurst. 1864. $10

THERE'S SOMETHING IN THE AIR. Adamson & McHugh. 1936. $1

THESE THINGS ARE YOU. Gannon & Kent. 1948. $1

THEY MADE IT TWICE AS NICE AND THEY CALLED IT DIXIELAND. Egan & Whiting. 1916. $2

THEY'RE COMING BACK. Sam Habelow. 1919. $2

(THE) THINGS I LOVE. Barlow & Harris. 1941. $1

THINGS WE WANT MOST ARE HARD TO GET. Meyer, Bryan & Laughlin. 1929. $2

THIS IS HEAVEN. Yellen & Akst. 1929. $2

THIS IS WORTH FIGHTING FOR. DeLange & Stept. 1942. $1

THIS YEAR'S KISSES. Irving Berlin. 1937. $2

THOMAS A. EDISON, MIRACLE MAN. Geo. M. Cohan. 1929. $9

THOSE CHARLIE CHAPLIN FEET. Leslie & Gottler. 1915. $3

THOSE RAGTIME MELODIES. G. Hodgkins. 1912. $16

THOU SHALT NOT! Gottler & Gay. 1932. $2

THREE CHEERS. Haim & Friedman. 1918. $7

THREE WONDERFUL LETTERS FROM HOME. Goodwin, MacDonald & Hanley. 1918. $2

THREE O'CLOCK IN THE MORNING. Torriss & Roblede. 1921. $2

THREE'S A CROWD. Dubin & Warren. 1932. $2

TILL THE GOLDEN GATES OF HEAVEN ARE CLOSED FOREVERMORE. Parquest & Keithly. 1915. $2

TING-A-LING. Britt & Little. 1934. $1

TIP TOE THROUGH THE TULIPS WITH ME. Dubin & Burke. 1929. $2

TIPPECANOE. Williams & Van Alstyne. 1904. $3

TO EACH HIS OWN. Livingston & Evans. 1946. $1

TO HAVE, TO HOLD, TO LOVE. MacBoyle & Ball. 1913. $2

TO YOU. Davis, Dorsey & Shapiro. 1939. $1

TOM, DICK, HARRY AND JACK. Johnson & Ager. 1917. $2

TOMAHAWK. J.A. McMeekin. 1916. $2

TOMMY. Taylor & Ramsay. 1904. $6

TONIGHT I'M GONNA SEE BABY. Raleigh & Wayne. 1943. $1

TONIGHT WILL LIVE. Washington & Lara. 1938. $1

TOO LATE NOW. Lerner & Lane. 1950. $1

TOO MARVELOUS FOR WORDS. Mercer & Whiting. 1937. $2

TOO OLD TO CUT THE MUSTARD. Dietrich & Clooney. 1951. $1

TOOLIE, OOLIE, DOOLIE. Horton & Beve. 1948. $1

TOOT TOOT TOOTSIE GOODBYE. Kahn, Erdman & Russo. 1949. $2

TRAMP, TRAMP, TRAMP. G. F. Root. 1864. $30

(A) TREE IN THE MEADOW. Billy Reid. 1947. $2

(A) TREE WAS A TREE. Gordon & Revel. 1933. $2

TRIPPING THRU THE DAISIES. W. F. Sudds. 1905. $4

TRIPOLI. Cunningham & Dubin. 1920. $2

(THE) TROJAN QUICK STEP. John C. Andrews. 1845. $42

TROPICAL SOUTH SEA ISLE. Wm. Friedlander. 1922. $2

TRUE. Samuels & Whitcup. 1934. $2

TRUE CONFESSIONS. Coslow & Hallander. 1938. $1

TRUE LOVE. Cole Porter. 1956. $1

(A) TRUE STORY. H.W. Loomis. 1923. $4

TRUST IN ME. Wever, Schwartz & Ager. 1936. $1

TUCK ME TO SLEEP IN MY OLD 'TUCKY HOME. Young & Lewis. 1921. $2

TURKISH MARCH. Beethoven, Rubinstein & Dioter. 1938. $1

TWELVE O'CLOCK WALTZ. Rose, Dixon & Warren. 1928. $2

TWILIGHT. McDonald & Lloyd. 1908. $4

TWO IN LOVE. Meredith Willson. 1941. $1

TWO SLEEPY PEOPLE. Loesser & Carmichael. 1938. $2

TWO TOGETHER. Kahn & Johnston. 1935. $3

TY-TEE (TAHITI). Wood & Bibo. 1921. $2

UNCHAINED MELODY. Zaret & North. 1935. $1

UNCLE SAMMY. Abe Holzmann. 1904. $4

UNDER THE CRESCENT. Shipman & Bull. 1915. $3

UNDER THE EVENING STAR. Ehrlich & Wenrich. 1908. $3

UNDER THE MOON. Lyn, Wheeler & Snyder. 1927. $2

UNDERNEATH THE HARLEM MOON. Gordon & Revel. 1932. $3

UPIDEE. Oliver Ditson. 1859. $26

UPSTAIRS & DOWN. Lewis, Young, & Donaldson. 1919. $2

(THE) VAGABOND KING WALTZ. Friml & Hooker. 1926. $2

VALSE ANGELIQUE. J. Brymm. 1913. $3

VICTORY. Wilson, Bard & Jerome. 1918. $3

VIENI-VIENI. Koger, Varma, Valley & Scott. 1934. $2

VIOLINS WERE PLAYING. Kenny & Silver. 1943. $1

VIRGINIA. Chas. Keyes. 1907. $3

VIRGINIA. Wilbur & Kent. 1911. $2

VIVE LA FRANCE. Warren & Dubin. 1934. $2

VO-DO-DE-O. Yellen & Ager. 1927. $1

WAIT FOR ME WHERE THE LILACS BLOOM. Arthur Lamb. 1905. $4

WAIT LOVE UNTIL THE WAR IS OVER. T. M. Todd. 1859. $40

WAITIN' AT THE GATE FOR KATEY. Kahn & Whiting. 1934. $3

WAITING FOR A CERTAIN GIRL. Richard Carle. 1906. $3

WAITING FOR THE ROBERT E. LEE. Gilbert & Muir. 1939. $1

WAITN' FOR THE MOON. O'Beil & Story. 1910. $2

WALKIN' MY BABY BACK HOME. Turk & Ahlert. 1930. $2

WALKING WITH SUSIE. Conrad. 1929. $2

WALTZ ME TILL I'M WEARY, DEARIE. Lonbrahe & Sherman. 1910. $2

(THE) WALTZ YOU SAVED FOR ME. Kahn, King & Flindt. 1930. $2

WARM AS WINE. Livingston & Evans. 1946. $1

(A) WARM RECEPTION. Bert Anthony. 1899. $10

WAS I A FOOL? Chas. Harris. 1909. $3

WAS IT RAIN. Hirsch & Handman. 1937. $1

WASHINGTON PIE. Ted Morse. 1907. $12

WATCH YOUR STEP. Geo. Becker. 1913. $2

WAY DOWN IN CAIRO. Stephen Foster. 1850. $25

WAY OUT WEST IN KANSAS. Carson Robinson. 1924. $2

(THE) WAY YOU LOOK TONIGHT. Kern & Fields. 1936. $1

WE DON'T KNOW WHERE WE'RE GOING BUT WE'RE ON OUR WAY. Williams. 1917. $5

WE JUST COULDN'T SAY GOODBYE. Harry Woods. 1932. $1

WE MUSTN'T SAY GOODBYE. Dubin & Monaco. 1943. $2

(THE) WEARING OF THE GREEN. House & Boucicoult's. 1865. $25

(THE) WEB OF LOVE. McNamee & Zany. 1929. $2

(THE) WEDDING OF THE PAINTED DOLL. Freed & Brown. 1929. $2

WEE, WEE MARIE. Bryan, McCarthy & Fisher. 1918. $2

WE'LL ALWAYS BE THE SAME SWEETHEARTS. Newman & Williams. 1911. $3

WE'LL MAKE HAY WHILE THE SUN SHINES. Freed & Brown. 1933. $2

WE'RE GOING OVER. Sterling, Grossman & Lange. 1917. $2

WEST VIRGINIA. Pack & Adderly. 1914. $3

WE'VE KEPT THE GOLDEN RULE. Deely & Wenrich. 1910. $4

WHAT A NIGHT, WHAT A MOON, WHAT A GIRL. John Loeb. 1935. $2

WHAT A WONDERFUL LOVE THAT WOULD BE. Whiting, Cunningham & Doyle. 1914. $3

WHAT ARE THE WILD WAVES SAYING? Stephen Glover. 1850. $16

WHAT ARE YOU DOING TO HELP THE BOYS? Kahn & Van Alstyne. 1918. $3

WHAT HAVE WE GOT TO LOSE. Kahn, Kent & Alter. 1933. $1

WHAT IS THIS THING CALLED LOVE? Cole Porter. 1929. $2

WHAT WILL I TELL MY HEART? Tinturin & Lawrence. 1937. $4

WHAT YOU GOING TO DO WHEN THE RENT COMES 'ROUND. Sterling & Von Tilzer. $2

WHAT'LL I DO. Irving Berlin. 1923. $2

WHAT'LL YOU DO? Cohn & Miller. 1927. $1

WHAT'S NEW? Burke & Haggart. 1939. $1

WHAT'S THE MATTER WITH FATHER. Williams & Van Alstyne. 1910. $3

WHEN I AM HOUSEKEEPING FOR YOU. Howard & Godron. 1929. $2

WHEN I COME BACK TO YOU. Tracey & Stern. 1918. $2

WHEN I DREAM IN THE GLOAMING OF YOU. Herbert Ingraham. 1909. $2

WHEN I GROWN TO BE A MAN. Rooney, Broderick & Dick. 1936. $1

WHEN I GROW TOO OLD TO DREAM. Hammerstein & Romberg. 1935. $2

WHEN I LOST YOU. Irving Berlin. 1912. $5

WHEN I MET YOU LAST NIGHT IN DREAMLAND. Whitson & Williams. 1911. $2

WHEN I SAID GOODBYE TO YOU. Max Friedman. 1923. $2

WHEN I SAW THAT SPANISH DANCER. Cox & Flatow. 1918. $2

WHEN I WALTZ WITH YOU. Bryan & Gumble. 1912. $5

WHEN I WAS A GIRL 18 YEARS OLD. John Cole. 1855. $17

WHEN I WAS QUITTING NORMAN BOWERS. Meyerbeer. 1850. $20

WHEN IT'S APPLE BLOSSOM TIME IN NORMANDIE. Gifford & Treator. 1912. $2

WHEN IT'S MOONLIGHT ON THE MISSISSIPPI. Vandeveer & Lange. 1915. $2

WHEN IT'S NIGHT TIME DOWN IN OLD DIXIELAND. Irving Berlin. 1912. $6

WHEN IT'S SPRINGTIME IN VIRGINIA. Walsh & Erdman. 1913. $2

WHEN JOHNNY COMES MARCHING HOME. Louis Lambert. 1863. $30

WHEN MOTHER NATURE SINGS HER LULLABY. Yoell & Brown. 1938. $2

WHEN MY DREAMS COME TRUE. Irving Berlin. 1929. $2

WHEN SHALL WE MEET AGAIN. Egan & Whiting. 1921. $2

WHEN THAT MIDNIGHT CHOO CHOO LEAVES FOR ALABAM'. Irving Berlin. 1912. $3

WHEN THE BOYS COME HOME. Hay & Speaks. 1917. $2

WHEN THE HARBOR LIGHTS ARE BURNING. Bryan & Solman. 1907. $5

WHEN THE HARVEST DAYS ARE OVER. Graham & Von Tilzer. 1900. $7

WHEN THE HARVEST MOON IS SHINING ON THE RIVER. Lamb & Henry. 1904. $3

WHEN THE LIGHTS GO ON AGAIN. Seiler, Marcus & Benjamin. 1942. $2

WHEN THE MOCKING BIRDS ARE SINGING IN THE WILDWOOD. Lambe & Blank. 1960. $3

WHEN THE MOON COMES OVER THE MOUNTAIN. Smith, Johnson & Woods. 1931. $3

WHEN THE ONE YOU LOVE LOVES YOU. Whiteman, Fried & Baer. 1924. $2

WHEN THE POPPIES BLOOM AGAIN. Towers, Morrow & Pelosi. 1936. $2

WHEN THE REAL THING COMES YOUR WAY. Larry Spier. 1929. $2

WHEN THE SUN GOES DOWN IN CAIRO TOWN. Black & Fisher. 1920. $2

WHEN THE SUNSET TURNS THE OCEAN'S BLUE TO GOLD. Buckner & Petrie. 1902. $3

WHEN THE TWILIGHT COMES TO KISS THE ROSE GOODNIGHT. Roden & Petrie. 1912. $2

WHEN THE WORLD IS AT REST. Davis & Fain. 1929. $1

WHEN THE YANKS COME MARCHING HOME. Jerome & Furth. 1918. $2

WHEN UNCLE JOE STEPS INTO FRANCE. Grossman & Winkle. 1918. $2

WHEN WE MEET IN THE SWEET BYE AND BYE. Stanley & Murphy. 1918. $2

WHEN WE REACH THAT OLD PORT SOMEWHERE IN FRANCE. Delden & Stept. 1917. $2

WHEN WE WERE TWO LITTLE BOYS. Madder & Morse. 1903. $3

WHEN WILL THE SUN SHINE FOR ME. Davis & Silver. 1923. $3

WHEN WORK IS THROUGH. Al Sherman. 1932. $2

WHEN YANKEE DOODLE LEARNS TO PARLEZ-VOUS FRANCAIS. Hart & Nelson. 1917. $2

WHEN YOU AND I WERE SEVENTEEN. Kahn & Rosoff. 1925. $1

WHEN YOU ARE OLD AND GRAY. Richard C. Dillmore. 1906. $2

WHEN YOU HEAR YOUR COUNTRY CALL. Geo. Colgan. 1914. $2

WHEN YOU HOLD ME IN YOUR ARMS. Buchanan & Klick. 1919. $2

WHEN YOU SANG HUSH A BYE BABY TO ME. Glick, Logan & Olman. 1918. $2

WHEN YOU'RE A LONG LONG WAY FROM HOME. Lewis & Meyer. 1914. $2

WHEN YOU'RE AWAY. Herbert & Blossom. 1914. $2

WHEN YOU'RE WITH SOMEBODY ELSE. Gilbert, Etting & Baer. 1927. $2

WHERE DID ROBINSON CRUSOE GO WITH FRIDAY ON SATURDAY NIGHT? Lewis, Young & Meyer. 1916. $2

WHERE HAVE WE MET BEFORE? Harburg, Duke & Perelman. 1932. $2

WHERE IS THE SONG OF SONGS FOR ME? Irving Berlin. 1928. $2

WHERE ROLLS THE OREGON. Boyle & Costa. 1916. $3

WHERE THE HUCKLEBERRIES GROW. Bryan, Richman & Silver. 1925. $2

WHERE THE HUDSON RIVER FLOWS. Jerome, Goetz & Gottler. 1915. $2
WHERE THE LAZY DAISIES GROW. Cliff Friend. 1924. $2
WHERE THE LAZY RIVER GOES BY. Adamson & McHugh. 1936. $2
WHERE THE RED RED ROSES GROW. Jerome & Schwartz. 1913. $3
WHERE THE RIVER SHANNON FLOWS. James Russell. 1906. $3
WHERE THE SHY LITTLE VIOLETS GROW. Warren & Kahn. 1925. $2
WHERE THE SOUTHERN ROSES GROW. Buck & Morse. 1904. $4
WHERE THE SWEET FORGET-ME-NOTS REMEMBER. Dixon & Warren. 1929. $2
WHILE A CIGARETTE WAS BURNING. Charles & Nick Kenny. 1938. $1
WHILE RIVERS OF LOVE FLOW ON. Graff & Ball. 1913. $4
WHILE STROLLING THROUGH THE PARK. Ed. Haley. 1939. $1
WHILE THE REST OF THE WORLD IS SLEEPING. Tobias, Rich & De Rose. 1933. $1
WHILE YOU'RE AWAY. Gilbert & Friedland. 1918. $2
WHISPER TO ME IN DREAMLAND. Smith & Lyons. 1924. $2
(A) WHISPERED THOUGHT. Chas. L. Johnson. 1904. $7
WHISPERING. Shoenberger, Coburn & Rose. 1920. $2
WHISPERING TREES, MEMORIES AND YOU. Wendell Hall. 1922. $1
WHISTLING RUFUS. Kerry Mills. 1899. $6
WHITE CHRISTMAS. Irving Berlin. 1942. $2
(THE) WHITE DOVE. Grey & Lehar. 1930. $2
WHOA, IDA, WHOA. Sterling & Von Tilzer. 1906. $3
WHO CAN TELL. Lebaren & Kreisler. 1919. $2
WHO TOLD YOU I CARED. Whiting & Reisfeld. 1930. $1
WHO WOULDN'T LOVE YOU. Carey & Fischer. 1942. $1
(THE) WHOLE WORLD IS SINGING MY SONG. Curtis & Mizzy. 1946. $1
WHO'LL BUY MY VIOLETS. Goetz & Padilla. 1923. $2
WHO'LL TAKE THE PLACE OF MARY. Dubin, Gaskil & Maye. 1920. $2
WHO'LL TAKE YOUR PLACE. Capano Carcik. 1935. $1
WHO-OO? YOU-OO! THAT'S WHO. Yellen & Ager. 1927. $2
WHOSE IZZY IS HE? Brown, Green & Sturn. 1924. $1
WHO'S AFRAID OF THE BIG BAD WOLF? Churchill & Ronell. 1933. $2
WHO'S THAT KNOCKING AT MY HEART? Freed & Lane. 1936. $1
WHY CAN'T I BE LIKE YOU? Conrad. 1929. $3
WHY COULDN'T IT BE POOR LITTLE ME? Kahn & Jones. 1924. $1
WHY COULDN'T IT LAST LAST NIGHT. Kenny, Henry & Croom. 1939. $1
WHY DID I KISS THAT GIRL? Brown, King & Henderson. 1924. $1
WHY DID IT HAVE TO BE ME. Gleen, Lombardo & Stept. 1931. $1
WHY DID YOU? Lombardo & Nippel. 1929. $1
WHY DID YOU LEAVE ME? Perry & Friedman. 1920. $2
WHY DO I LOVE YOU? Hammerstein & Kern. 1927. $1
WHY DON'T THEY SET HIM FREE? Blue & Loll. 1913. $4
WHY DON'T YOU SPEAK FOR YOURSELF, JOHN? Corinne & Ross. 1923. $2
WHY SHOULD I GIVE MY HEART TO YOU. Davis & Brookhoise. 1916. $2
WILD FLOWER. Martens & Eral. 1920. $2
WILD ROSE. Donart & Webster. 1909. $3

WILL YOU REMEMBER ME. Davis, Santly & Richmon. 1924. $1

(THE) WIND IN THE TREES. Betty Boutelle. 1931. $1

(THE) WINDS BLOW FREE. Tyson & Leshner. 1941. $1

WINTER. Bryan & Gumble. 1910. $3

WISH ME GOOD LUCK, KISS ME GOOD BYE. Davis & Ager. 1934. $1

WISHING. DeSylva. 1939. $3

WISHING AND WAITING FOR LOVE. Clarke & Akst. 1929. $2

WITH ALL MY HEART. Kahn & McHugh. 1935. $5

WITH EVERY BREATH I TAKE. Robin & Rainger. 1934. $2

WITHERED ROSES. Garland, Shay & Gillespie. 1928. $2

WITHOUT A SONG. Youmans, Rose & Ellison. 1929. $4

WITHOUT A WORD OF WARNING. Gordon & Revel. 1935. $2

WONDERFUL ONE. Terriss, Whiteman & Grofe. 1923. $2

WON'T YOU COME OVER TO PHILLY, WILLY? Gardenier & Helf. 1907. $2

WON'T YOU LET ME TAKE YOU HOME? Doerr & Lashly. 1912. $3

WON'T YOU MEET ME OUT IN WICHITA. Fleta Jan Brown. 1914. $2

WON'T YOU PROMISE ME. Arthur Williams. 1918. $2

WOODY WOODPECKER. Tibbles & Iriss. 1948. $2

(THE) WORDS ARE IN MY HEART. Dubin & Warren. $1

(THE) WORST IS YET TO COME. Lewis, Young & Grant. 1918. $4

WOULD YOU LIKE TO TAKE A WALK? Dixon, Rose & Warren. 1930. $2

WOULD YOU TAKE ME BACK AGAIN? Lamb & Solman. 1913. $3

WOULDN'T IT BE WONDERFUL. Clarke & Akst. 1929. $2

YANKEE DOODLE. Dr. Schackburg. 1942. $1

(THE) YANKEE DOODLE BOY. Geo. M. Cohan. 1904. $6

YANKEE ROSE. Holden & Frankl. 1926. $1

(THE) YANKS ARE AT IT AGAIN. Brown & Cowan. 1918. $3

YEARNING. Davis & Burke. 1925. $2

YOO HOO. DeSylva & Jolson. 1912. $3

YO TO AMO MEANS I LOVE YOU. Whiting & Bryan. 1928. $2

YOU. Adamson & Donaldson. 1936. $2

YOU AND I. Meredith Wilson. 1941. $1

YOU APPEAL TO ME. Bullock & Spina. 1938. $2

YOU ARE CHILDREN OF THE USA. Van Every & Conrad. 1917. $2

YOU ARE MY LUCKY STAR. Freed & Brown. 1935. $1

YOU ARE THE MUSIC TO THE WORDS IN MY HEART. Pokrass & Yellen. 1938. $1

YOU ARE THE ONE AND ONLY. Clare Kummer. 1913. $3

YOU ARE TOO BEAUTIFUL. Rodgers & Hart. 1945. $1

YOU BELONG TO ME I BELONG TO YOU. Newman & Lombardo. 1929. $2

YOU BROUGHT ME LOVE. Hastings & Ross. 1919. $1

YOU BUY AND I'LL BUY MORE WAR SAVINGS STAMPS. Eddie Mallery. 1918. $5

YOU CAME TO MY RESCUE. Robin & Rainger. 1936. $2

YOU CAN'T MAKE A FOOL OUT OF ME. Cunningham & Van Alstyne. 1923. $1

YOU CAN'T SAY NO TO A SOLDIER. Gordon & Warren. 1942. $1

YOU CAN'T STOP ME FROM DREAMING. Friend & Franklin. 1937. $1

YOU CAN'T STOP THE YANKS. Caddigan & Story. 1918. $2

YOU DARLIN'. Harry Woods. 1930. $2

YOU DIDN'T KNOW ME FROM ADAM. Burke & Loeb. 1934. $2

YOU FORGOT YOUR GLOVES. Henry & Hamilton. 1931. $2

YOU GOT THE BEST OF ME. Joe Fant. 1941. $1

YOU HIT THE SPOT. Gordon & Revel. 1935. $2

YOU KNOW YOU BELONG TO SOMEBODY ELSE. West & Monaco. 1922. $3

YOU LOOK GOOD TO ME. Rose & Donaldson. 1938. $2

YOU MADE ME CARE. Jos. Gilbert. 1939. $2

YOU MIGHT HAVE BELONGED TO ANOTHER. West & Harmon. 1941. $1

YOU MUST BELIEVE ME. Tobias & Burke. 1933. $2

YOU MUST HAVE BEEN A BEAUTIFUL BABY. Warren & Mercer. 1938. $1

YOU NEVER LOOKED SO BEAUTIFUL. Donaldson & Adamson. 1936. $1

YOU OR NO ONE. Rothberg & Tinturin. 1933. $1

Y-O-U SPELLS THE ONE I LOVE. Harris & Melsher. 1938. $1

YOU TOLD ME. Sedgwick, Lyman & Cohen. 1925. $1

YOU TOOK ADVANTAGE OF ME. Rodgers & Hart. 1928. $2

YOU TOOK THE WORDS RIGHT OUT OF MY HEART. Robin & Rainger. 1938. $1

YOU WAITED TOO LONG. Autry, Whitley & Rose. 1940. $1

YOU YOU DARLIN'. Scholl & Jerome. 1940. $1

YOU'D BE SO NICE TO COME HOME TO. Cole Porter. 1942. $1

YOU'D BE SURPRISED. Irving Berlin. 1919. $4

YOU'LL BE REMINDED OF ME. Jessel, Meskill & Shapiro. 1938. $1

YOU'LL BE SORRY. Maceo Pinkard. 1919. $1

YOU'LL BE THERE. Brennan & Ball. 1915. $7

YOU'LL BE THERE TO MEET THEM. Branon & Heinrich. 1918. $2

YOU'LL NEVER GET UP TO HEAVEN THAT WAY. Lerner & Baer. 1933. $2

YOU'LL NEVER KNOW. Gordon, Warren & Rose. 1943. $1

YOUNG AMERICA, WE'RE STRONG FOR YOU! Wm. McKenna. 1915. $2

YOUNG EPH'S LAMENT. Murphy & Purdy. 1863. $35

YOUR COUNTRY NEEDS YOU NOW. Rubin, Carmack & McConnell. 1917. $2

YOU'RE A MILLION MILES FROM NOWHERE. Donaldson, Young & Lewis. 1919. $1

YOU'RE A REAL SWEETHEART. Caesar & Friend. 1928. $2

YOU'RE A SWEET LITTLE HEADACHE. Robin & Rainger. 1928. $3

YOU'RE ALWAYS IN MY ARMS. McCarthy & Tierney. 1929. $2

YOU'RE ALL I NEED. Kahn. 1935. $1

YOU'RE BEAUTIFUL TONIGHT MY DEAR. Young & Lombardo. 1933. $2

YOU'RE DRIVING ME CRAZY. Walter Donaldson. 1930. $1

YOU'RE HERE AND I'M HERE. Smith & Kern. 1914. $2

YOU'RE MY PAST, PRESENT AND FUTURE. Gordon & Revel. 1933. $1

YOU'RE STILL AN OLD SWEETHEART OF MINE. Egan & Whiting. 1918. $2

YOURS AND MINE. Nelson & Burke. 1930. $2

YOURS AND MINE. Freed & Brown. 1938. $1

YOU'VE GOTTA EAT YOUR SPINACH, BABY. Gordon & Revel. 1936. $1

YPSILANTI. Bryan & Van Alstyne. 1915. $2

ZAMBESI. Hilliard, DeWall & Carstens. 1955. $1

CHAPTER XII

Bibliography

Ascap Biographical Dictionary of Composers, Authors, and Publishers. Rev. ed. New York: T.Y. Crowell, 1952.

Ascap Index of Performed Compositions. 3 vols. New York: Ascap, 1963.

Burton, Jack. *The Blue Book of Tin Pan Alley.* Watkins Glen, N.Y.: Century House, 1950.

Burton, Jack. *Index of American Popular Music.* Watkins Glen, N.Y.: Century House, 1957.

Chipman, John H. *Index to Top-Hit Tunes.* Boston: Bruce Humphries, 1962.

Dichter, Harry and Shapiro, Eliot. *Early American Sheet Music: Its Lure and Lore.* New York: R.W. Bowker, 1941.

Dumont, Frank. *The Witmark Amateur Minstrel Guide and Burnt Cork Encyclopedia.* Rev. ed. New York: M. Witmark, 1927.

Ewen, David. *American Popular Songs.* New York: Random House, 1965.

Ewen, David. *History of Popular Music.* New York: Barnes and Noble, 1961.

Ewen, David. *The Life and Death of Tin Pan Alley.* New York: Funk and Wagnalls, 1964.

Gilbert, Douglas. *Lost Chords.* New York: Doubleday Doran, 1942.

Goldberg, Isaac. *Tin Pan Alley.* New York: Day Co., 1930.

Harris, Charles. *After the Ball: Forty Years of Melody.* New York: Frank Maurice, 1926.

Howard, John Tasker. *Our American Music.* New York: T.Y. Crowell, 1946.

Klamkin, Marian. *Old Sheet Music.* New York: Hawthorne, 1975.

Kenny, Nick. *How to Write and Sell Popular Songs.* New York: Hermitage Press, 1946.

Levy, Lester S. *Grace Notes in American History.* Norman, Okla.: Univ. of Oklahoma Press, 1967.

Loesser, Arthur, *Men, Women and Pianos.* New York: Simon and Shuster, 1954.

Marcuse, Frank. *Tin Pan Alley in Gaslight.* Watkins Glen, N.Y.: Century House, 1959.

Marks, Edward B. *They All Sang.* New York: Viking, 1934.

Meyer, Hazel. *The Gold in Tin Pan Alley.* Philadelphia: J.P. Lippincott, 1958.

Shemel, Sidney and Krasilovsky, M.W. *This Business of Music.* Edited by Paul Ackerman. New York: Billboard Publications, 1971.

Spaeth, Sigmund. *A History of Popular Music.* New York: Random House, 1948.

Stecheson, Anthony and Stecheson, Ann. *Classified Song Directory.* Hollywood, Calif.: Music Industry Publications, 1961.

Westin, Helen. *Introducing the Song Sheet.* Nashville, Tenn.: Nelson, 1976.

Witmark, Isadore and Goldberg, Isaac. *From Ragtime to Swingtime.* New York: Lee Furman, 1939.

Witmark, Isadore and Goldberg, Isaac. *The Story of the House of Witmark.* New York: Lee Furman, 1939.